THE BUXTED
POULTRY
COOKBOOK

THE BUXTED
POULTRY
COOKBOOK

ENNIS OTTER

Lyric

CONTENTS

First published 1979 by Lyric Books Ltd.
66b The Broadway, London NW7

© 1979 Lyric Books Ltd.
Text © 1979 Buxted Poultry Ltd.

Reprinted 1979

ISBN 0 7111 0001 2
Printed in Great Britain by
Severn Valley Press Ltd.

INTRODUCTION

As well as tasting delicious, frozen poultry is one of the most nourishing foods available. High in body-building protein, but low in fat and calories it is a truly valuable part of our diet. Chicken is 29% protein and contains more protein per ounce than cheese, beef, eggs or milk.

It is versatile too, as the tender flesh of poultry can mix with many other flavours to produce countless different dishes — economically, too, because poultry is such good value for money.

TYPES OF CHICKEN AVAILABLE

New York Dressed is an historic term to describe chicken which is sold fresh-killed in butchers, without being gutted, drawn or cleaned. The chicken is displayed with all body feathers removed and once you have purchased it, your butcher will normally gut and clean the bird for you.

Oven-ready fresh chickens are completely cleaned and are normally sold chilled.

Frozen poultry is first cleaned and then frozen. It is a convenient way of buying chicken as it is readily available and can be kept in the home freezer.

Poussins are 4-6 weeks old, weighing about 1lb (0.5kg). Usually serve one person and are either fresh or frozen.

Boiling hens, 2½-7lb (1-3kg), previously egg-layers or broiler breeders. They come oven-ready or New York Dressed.

6

Chicken

THAWING TIMES

Weight	Thawed at Room Temperature 65°F(18°C)	Thawed in Refrigerator
2lbs (1kg)	8 hours	28 hours
3lbs (1.25kg)	9 hours	32 hours
4lbs (1.75kg)	10 hours	38 hours
5lbs (2.25kg)	12 hours	44 hours
6lbs (2.5kg)	14 hours	50 hours
7lbs (3kg)	16 hours	56 hours

Q. How long can I store frozen chickens in my freezer?

A. Up to three months.

SERVINGS AND COOKING TIMES

Servings	Weight
3	3lb (1.25kg)
4	3½lb (1.25-1.5kg)
5	4lb (1.75kg)
6	4½-5lb (2-2.25kg)

Average cooking times for roast chicken are 20 minutes to the pound plus 20 minutes at 375°F (190°C, Gas Mark 5).

When roasting poultry, the use of foil helps to retain the bird's natural juices, reduces the need for basting and keeps the meat deliciously tender. Using foil takes the same time to cook but requires a slightly higher oven temperature. Place foil loosely over the bird, and roast at 425°F (220°C, Gas Mark 7) for 20 minutes per pound plus 20 minutes or until the bird is cooked. Remove the foil for the last 20 minutes to allow the bird to brown.

To test when your chicken is cooked, insert a skewer or pointed knife into the thickest part of the thigh. If the juices that run out are clear, then the bird is cooked. If they are not, continue cooking for another 10 minutes or so and test again.

Turkey

THAWING TIMES

Weight	Thawed at Room Temperature 65°F (18°C)	Thawed in Refrigerator 40°F (4°C)	Weight	Thawed at Room Temperature 65°F (18°C)	Thawed in Refrigerator 40°F (4°C)
5- 6lbs (2.25-2.5kg)	18-20 hours	40-50 hours	17-20lbs (7.5-8.75kg)	33-35 hours	78-82 hours
6- 8lbs (2.75-3.5kg)	20-23 hours	50-60 hours	20-25lbs (8.75-11kg)	35-40 hours	82-86 hours
8-10lbs (3.5-8kg)	23-26 hours	60-66 hours			
10-12lbs (4.5-5.25kg)	26-29 hours	66-70 hours			
12-15lbs (5.25-6.5kg)	29-31 hours	70-74 hours			
15-17lbs (6.5-7.5kg)	31-33 hours	74-78 hours			

N.B. Thaw all turkeys in the bag but not in the box. Remove the giblets and neck from the turkey as soon as they are free, as this aids thawing. Keep the turkey covered when the bag is removed to prevent drying out on the surface.

SERVINGS AND COOKING TIMES

Servings	Weight	Unstuffed or Neck Stuffed Cooked at 325°F (160°C, Gas Mark 3)	Fully Stuffed 20 mins at 400°F (200°C, Gas Mark 6) and then at 350°F (180°C, Gas Mark 4)
6-8	5-6lbs (2.25-2.5kg)	3-3½ hours	3-3½ hours
8-12	6-8lbs (2.7-3.5kg)	3½-4 hours	3½-4 hours
	8-10lbs (3.5-4.5kg)	4-4½ hours	4-4½ hours
13-15	10-12lbs (4.5-5.25kg)	4½-5 hours	4½-5 hours
	12-15lbs (5.25-6.5kg)	5-5½ hours	5-5½ hours
20-30	15-17lbs (6.5-7.5kg)	5½-6 hours	5½-6 hours
	17-20lbs (7.5-8.75kg)	6-6½ hours	6-6½ hours
40-45	20-25lbs (8.75-11kg)	6½-7½ hours	6½-7½ hours

Alternative Cooking Methods

Slow Cooker

Q. Can I use frozen poultry in a slow cooker?
A. Yes, provided it has completely thawed. Always cook whole birds on HIGH. Do not switch to LOW.

Slow cooking is not new. Our grandmothers used to leave casseroles cooking gently all day. With the slow cooker you are not tied to the kitchen, the meal requires no attention and will not stick, burn or boil over.

Pressure Cooking

Q. Is a whole chicken timed by weight in a pressure cooker?
A. Yes. The cooking time is calculated from the weight of the bird plus the stuffing, if stuffing is being used. More liquid is usually required to last the cooking time so the manufacturer's instruction book should be consulted.
Q. If I cook more than 4 pieces of chicken (for example, 8 pieces), do I have to increase the cooking time?
A. No. When cooking 'pieces' of poultry the cooking time remains the same whether you are cooking 2 pieces or 8 pieces.

Pressure cooking is economical and quick, but cooking times and pressures may vary from one make of cooker to another. Therefore you *must* follow the instructions for your individual pressure cooker.

Microwave

Q. Can I thaw frozen chickens using a microwave?

A. Yes. An approximate guide is 6 minutes per pound (0.5kg), but if you have an automatic defrost cycle on your microwave oven, then the following table is appropriate.
(The defrost cycle will give you so many minutes microwaving and then so many minutes "rest" period. This prevents the food from being almost cooked on the outside, but not defrosted properly inside). Using a defrost cycle:
For 2lb 12oz (1.2kg) chicken set timer to 24 minutes.
For 3lb (1.3kg) chicken set timer to 24 minutes.
For 3lb 4oz (1.4kg) chicken set timer to 24 minutes.
For 3lb 8oz (1.5kg) chicken set timer to 24 minutes.
For 3lb 12oz (1.6kg) chicken set timer to 30 minutes.
For 4lb (1.8kg) chicken set timer to 30 minutes.
Turn the chicken round every 10 minutes or so and remove the bag of giblets as soon as they become free.
After defrosting allow the chicken to stand at room temperature for 10-20 minutes before cooking.

Cooking Brick

Q. Do I have to soak the cooking brick?
A. Soak it in water for 15 minutes every time. When ready for cooking, put it in the oven, before you set it to the required temperature. Set oven at 275°F (140°C, Gas Mark 1) for 5 minutes and then gradually raise it until the desired temperature is reached.

Poultry cooks in its natural juices and the flavour and nutrients are retained. The food also requires no additional fat.

Roasting Bags

Q. Why should I flour the inside of my roasting bag and make slits in it before cooking?
A. The flour helps the self-basting, so that the food is a golden colour when cooked. It is important to make slits or the bag could explode during cooking. Always use the twist ties provided.

Roasting bags keep your oven clean, brown your food beautifully — no need to baste — and even the strongest food smells will not escape into the kitchen.

Cooking in a Parcel

Q. Should I use liquid when cooking in baking parchment?
A. No. The food cooks in its own juices, but you can add a little butter.
Q. Can I use any temperature when using foil?
A. Yes. Foil is ideal for heat up to 475°F (240°C, Gas Mark 9).

Boiling Bags

Q. What kind of chicken should I use in boiling bags?
A. Chicken quarters should be cooked but you can use diced raw chicken off the bone.
Q. Can boiling bags be subjected to extreme temperatures?
A. Yes, they are suitable for freezing and boiling.

COMPARATIVE OVEN TEMPERATURES

° Fahrenheit	° Centigrade	Gas Mark
150°F	70°C	
175°F	80°C	
200°F	100°C	
225°F	110°C	1/4
250°F	130°C	1/2
275°F	140°C	1
300°F	150°C	2
325°F	160°C	3
350°F	180°C	4
375°F	190°C	5
400°F	200°C	6
425°F	220°C	7
450°F	230°C	8
475°F	240°C	9
500°F	250°C	
525°F	270°C	
550°F	290°C	

GLOSSARY OF TERMS

Bake Blind — To bake without any filling, e.g. a pastry case.

Baste — To spoon hot fat or liquid over food as it cooks.

Blanch — To whiten meats and remove strong tastes from vegetables by plunging into boiling water for a few minutes, also used to remove skin from tomatoes etc. — see scald.

Bouquet Garni — Traditionally a bunch of parsley, thyme and bay leaf tied together and used for flavouring stews and sauces. Other herbs can be added. The bouquet garni is removed before serving.

Cocotte — 'En Cocotte' implies that the food is cooked and served in the same round or oval overproof dish.

Croûtons — Small cubes of fried bread which are served with purée or cream soups.

Infuse — To soak in liquid in a warm place to draw flavour into the liquid.

Liaison — Mixture for thickening or binding together a sauce, gravy or soup, e.g. roux, egg yolks, cream or butter and flour.

Marinate — To soak raw meat in a seasoned liquid of wine, oil, herbs and vegetables for several hours or days before cooking. This softens and flavours and the marinade can be used in the cooking or to make the final sauce.

Reduce — To boil down a liquid or sauce in order to concentrate flavour and thicken the consistency.

Refresh — To pour cold water over previously blanched and drained food.

Roux — Fat and flour liaison. The basis of all flour sauces.

Sauté — To brown food in oil, butter or margarine.

Scald — To plunge food into boiling water for easy peeling, e.g. tomatoes or to heat a liquid such as milk to just under boiling point.

Sweat — To cook diced or sliced vegetables gently in a little butter or other fat in a covered pan, in order to give flavour.

9

STEP-BY-STEP PREPARATION

CARVING

1. Hold bird firmly with carving fork through breast. Cut skin around the leg, place knife between leg and carcass, press gently outwards to expose the joint. Cut through, slipping under the back to release the oyster with thigh.

2. Hold knife at top of breast at neck end of bird and cut down parallel to one side of wishbone to cut a good slice of breast and wing. Repeat with other side of the chicken.

3. Carve remaining breast into slices following line of the carcass.

4. Divide the leg portions through the joint which joins the drumstick and thigh.

1

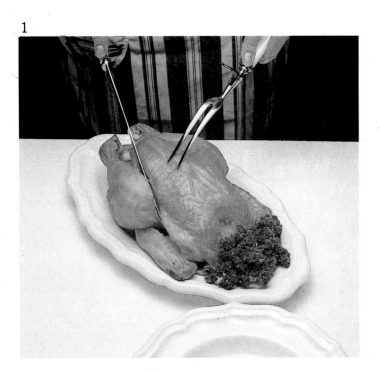

3

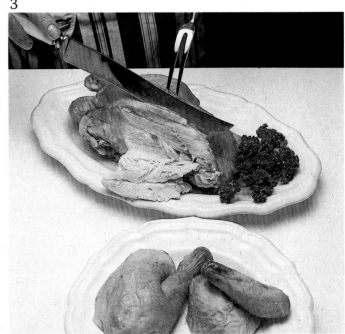

2

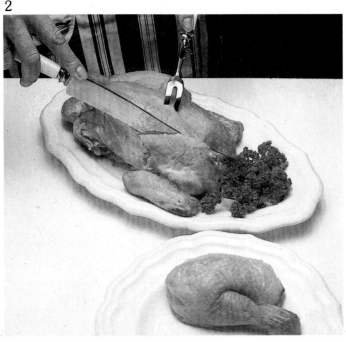

4

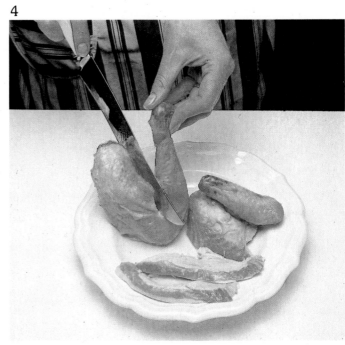

STUFFING AND TRUSSING

5. Spoon stuffing into neck-end of chicken. Fold neck flap over.

6. Using a barding needle or a large darning needle and thread, sew neck flap to carcass. Turn bird over and mould stuffing into a good shape.

7. Push a skewer through one wing, the neck flap and out through the other wing. Pass another skewer through the bird from one leg to the other.

8. Tie legs together with thread.

5

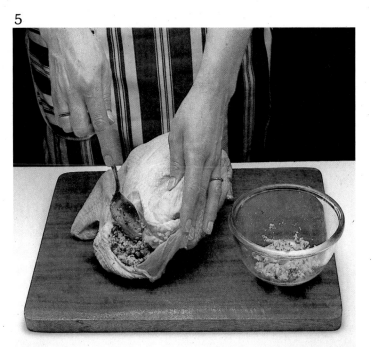

6

7

8

9. Cut the skin along backbone, using a sharp pointed knife.

10. Cut skin and flesh away from one side of carcass until leg joint is reached. Cut sinew between ball and socket joint joining thigh bone to carcass. Hold end of joint in one hand and working from inside of leg, cut away flesh and scrape thigh bone clean. Continue cleaning drumstick until both thigh and leg bone are free of flesh. Repeat with other leg and thigh.

11. Sever the wing joint from the carcass. Cut down towards the breastbone and scrape the wing bone clean. Repeat with other wing.

   Very carefully cut away skin from top of breastbone taking care not to nick the skin so that the chicken remains in one piece for stuffing.

12. Lay the boned out chicken flat. Fill with stuffing and sew up with needle and thread. Shape and truss.

9

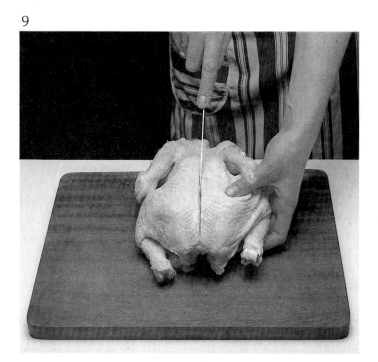

11

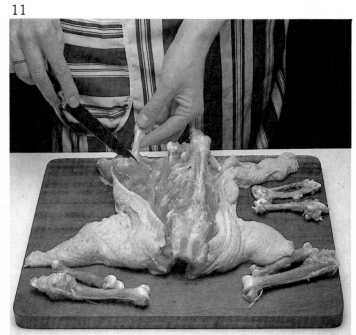

10

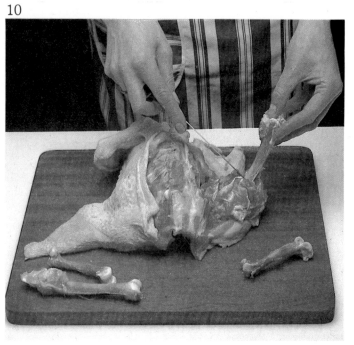

12

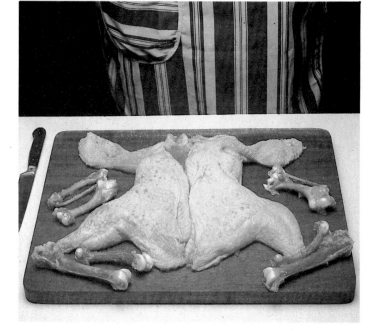

PORTIONING

13. Remove leaf-fat from inside carcass and cut off parson's nose. Cut off ends of wings and the shanks.

14. With poultry shears or a strong sharp knife cut lengthways along breast bone. Open bird out and cut through length of backbone.

15. Place knife between leg and carcass and cut through. Cut off wing taking a good slice of breast with it to make an equal portion. Repeat with other side of bird.

16. Divide the leg portions through the joint which joins the drumstick and thigh.

13

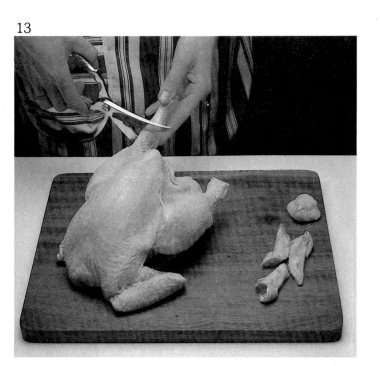

15

14

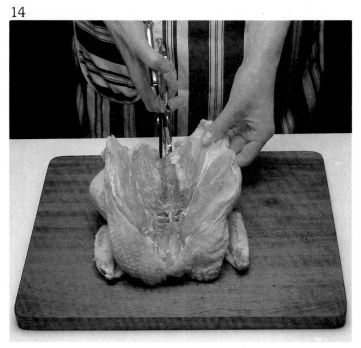

16

Soups and Starters

CHICKEN AND SORREL SOUP

Imperial	Metric
1 small onion, finely chopped	1 small onion, finely chopped
6oz fresh sorrel, washed and cut finely	150g fresh sorrel, washed and cut finely
2oz butter	50g butter
¾lb potatoes, peeled and sliced thinly	300g potatoes, peeled and sliced thinly
1½ pints chicken stock	850ml chicken stock
salt	salt
pepper	pepper
1 egg yolk beaten with 4 tablespoons single cream	1 egg yolk beaten with 4 tablespoons single cream
fried croûtons of bread to serve	fried croûtons of bread to serve

Serves four
Preparation time: 10 minutes
Cooking time: 45 minutes

Heat the butter, add the onion and sorrel, cook for a few minutes. Add the potatoes, stock and seasoning and bring to the boil. Cover and simmer gently for 30-35 minutes. Pass the soup through a vegetable mill or blend in an electric blender. Return the soup to pan, add the blended egg yolks and cream and heat gently. Adjust seasoning, and serve at once accompanied by the croûtons.

Left: Chicken and Sorrel Soup
Above centre: Vichyssoise
Below centre: Chicken and Rice Soup
Right: Iced Tomato Soup

CHICKEN AND RICE SOUP

Imperial	Metric
2oz butter or margarine	50g butter or margarine
1 large carrot, grated	1 large carrot, grated
1 medium onion, grated	1 medium onion, grated
1 medium potato, grated	1 medium potato, grated
2 celery stalks, finely chopped	2 celery stalks, finely chopped
2 pints chicken stock	1.2 litres chicken stock
salt	salt
pepper	pepper
2oz long-grain rice, washed in cold water	50g long-grain rice, washed in cold water

Serves four to six
Preparation time: 15 minutes
Cooking time: 20 to 25 minutes

Heat butter or margarine and fry the vegetables for 5 minutes without browning them. Add the chicken stock and seasoning, bring to the boil and then add the rice. Simmer for 20-25 minutes and serve.

VICHYSSOISE

Imperial	Metric
2oz butter	50g butter
2 leeks, thinly sliced	2 leeks, thinly sliced
1 medium onion, finely chopped	1 medium onion, finely chopped
1 stick celery, chopped	1 stick celery, chopped
1 medium potato, peeled and sliced	1 medium potato, peeled and sliced
salt	salt
pepper	pepper
1 pint chicken stock	575ml chicken stock
1 tablespoon chopped fresh parsley	1 tablespoon chopped fresh parsley
3fl oz single cream, chilled	75ml single cream, chilled
chopped chives	chopped chives

Serves four
Preparation time: 15 minutes
Cooking time: 30 minutes

Heat the butter, add the leeks and onion and cook slowly until transparent but not browned. Add celery, potato, seasoning and stock, cover pan and simmer for 20-30 minutes or until potatoes are cooked. Rub through a sieve or use an electric blender. Chill. Just before serving, stir in the parsley and cream. Serve in chilled bowls, with chives.

ICED TOMATO SOUP

Imperial	Metric
8oz potatoes, cooked until tender	225g potatoes, cooked until tender
¼ cucumber, peeled and roughly chopped	¼ cucumber, peeled and roughly chopped
1 small onion, peeled and roughly chopped	1 small onion, peeled and roughly chopped
1 clove garlic, peeled	1 clove garlic, peeled
8oz can tomatoes	225g can tomatoes
6-8 leaves fresh basil or ¼ teaspoon dried basil	6-8 leaves fresh basil or ¼ teaspoon dried basil
1½ pints chicken stock	850ml chicken stock
1 tablespoon tomato purée	1 tablespoon tomato purée
2 level teaspoons sugar	2 level teaspoons sugar
salt	salt
pepper	pepper
2 tablespoons double cream	2 tablespoons double cream

Serves four to six
Preparation time: 15 to 20 minutes

Blend the potatoes, cucumber, onion, garlic, tomatoes and basil together, then stir in the chicken stock, tomato purée, sugar and seasoning to taste. Cover and leave in refrigerator to chill thoroughly. Serve in individual bowls or a large tureen and swirl in the double cream.

Left: Cock-A-Leekie
Above centre: Cream of Chicken Soup
Below centre: Chinese Chicken Soup
Right: Golden Chicken Soup

CREAM OF CHICKEN SOUP

Imperial	Metric
2 pints chicken stock	1.25 litres chicken stock
2oz butter or margarine	50g butter or margarine
2oz flour	50g flour
salt	salt
pepper and a little grated nutmeg, if liked	pepper and a little grated nutmeg, if liked
¼ pint single cream or top of the milk	125ml single cream or top of the milk
2oz chicken meat taken from the carcass and cubed (optional)	50g chicken meat taken from the carcass and cubed (optional)
fried croûtons of bread to serve	fried croûtons of bread to serve

Serves four to six
Preparation time: 5 to 10 minutes
Cooking time: 10 to 15 minutes

Melt butter or margarine, add flour, cook for 1-2 minutes. Gradually add stock, stirring all the time. Bring to boil and then simmer for 2 minutes. Add the chicken meat (if used) and add the cream. Season to taste and heat through very gently. Serve at once accompanied by fried croûtons of bread.

CHINESE CHICKEN SOUP

Imperial	Metric
2 pints chicken stock	1.25 litres chicken stock
4oz button mushrooms, thinly sliced	100g button mushrooms, thinly sliced
3-4oz cooked chicken breast meat, thinly sliced	75-100g cooked chicken breast meat, thinly sliced
salt	salt
2oz bamboo shoots, thinly sliced (optional)	50g bamboo shoots, thinly sliced (optional)

Serves four to six
Cooking time: 15 minutes

Bring the broth to the boil, add the chicken and mushrooms and the bamboo shoots, if used. Season with salt to taste. Simmer for about 5 minutes, then serve immediately.

COCK-A-LEEKIE

Imperial	Metric
3½lb chicken	1.5kg chicken
4 pints water	2.25 litres water
2oz pearl barley	50g pearl barley
salt	salt
pepper	pepper
2lb leeks, thoroughly washed and sliced	1kg leeks, thoroughly washed and sliced
2oz prunes, soaked overnight, stoned and halved (optional)	50g prunes, soaked overnight, stoned and halved (optional)

Serves six to eight
Preparation time: 10 minutes
Cooking time: 1 hour 45 minutes

Put the chicken and ¾ of the leeks in a large pan with the water. Cover and bring to the boil, then simmer gently for about 1 hour or until the chicken is tender. Skim the soup then add the remaining leeks, the barley, seasoning and prunes (if used). Cover and continue simmering for 30 minutes. Take out the chicken and remove the meat, discarding the skin and bones. Cut the meat into ½-inch (1cm) cubes. Add the meat to the liquid and simmer for another 5 minutes. Serve with crusty bread.

GOLDEN CHICKEN SOUP

Imperial	Metric
Stock	**Stock**
1 chicken carcass with some meat left on it	1 chicken carcass with some meat left on it
1 onion cut in half	1 onion cut in half
1 bay leaf	1 bay leaf
1 teaspoon salt	1 teaspoon salt
1 bouquet garni	1 bouquet garni
Soup	**Soup**
1oz margarine	25g margarine
1 large onion, sliced	1 large onion, sliced
1 large potato, sliced	1 large potato, sliced
1 stick celery, or a shake of celery salt	1 stick celery, or a shake of celery salt
½lb carrots, sliced	225g carrots, sliced
salt	salt
pepper	pepper
chopped parsley for garnishing	chopped parsley for garnishing
fried croûtons of bread to serve	fried croûtons of bread to serve

Serves four to six
Preparation and cooking time for stock:
2 hours 10 minutes
Preparation and cooking time for soup: 25 minutes

Put carcass, onion, bay leaf, salt and bouquet garni into a large pan, cover with water, bring to the boil and simmer for about 2 hours. Strain stock and take off pieces of chicken meat from the bones and add to stock. If allowed to cool the fat can then be scooped off easily. Store in refrigerator until needed for soup. Melt margarine and lightly fry onion, potatoes, celery and carrots in it for about 5 minutes. Add stock and seasoning. Bring to boil and then simmer for about 20 minutes or until vegetables are tender. Blend in a liquidizer or put through a sieve and serve garnished with parsley and accompanied by fried croûtons of bread.

CUCUMBER SOUP

Imperial	Metric
1oz butter or margarine	25g butter or margarine
1 large cucumber, peeled and cut into chunks	1 large cucumber, peeled and cut into chunks
1 medium onion, sliced thinly	1 medium onion, sliced thinly
1 pint chicken stock	575ml chicken stock
salt	salt
pepper	pepper
¼ pint milk or single cream	125ml milk or single cream
1 tablespoon mint, chopped	1 tablespoon mint, chopped

Serves three to four
Preparation time: 10 minutes
Cooking time: 25 minutes

Heat butter and fry the onion until tender but without allowing it to brown. Add cucumber and stock, season to taste and simmer for 25 minutes. Put through a sieve or blend in electric blender. Allow to cool. Add milk or cream and chill thoroughly in refrigerator. Serve in chilled soup bowls and garnish with chopped mint.

DUCK SOUP

Imperial	Metric
2 duck carcasses	2 duck carcasses
1oz butter	25g butter
1 onion, sliced	1 onion, sliced
bouquet garni	bouquet garni
1 glass port	1 glass port
celery salt	celery salt
pepper	pepper
cayenne	cayenne

Preparation time: 10 minutes
Cooking time: 2 to 3 hours

Melt the butter, add sliced onion and cook gently. Add the broken carcasses and bouquet garni. Cover with water and simmer for 2-3 hours. Strain. Bring to the boil, then add the port and seasoning.

TURKEY SOUP

Imperial	Metric
turkey carcass	turkey carcass
bouquet garni	bouquet garni
8oz onions, chopped	225g onions, chopped
2oz margarine	50g margarine
8oz potatoes, diced	225g potatoes, diced
8oz carrots, diced	225g carrots, diced
3 sticks of celery, diced	3 sticks of celery, diced
salt	salt
pepper	pepper
2 bay leaves	2 bay leaves
2oz cornflour	50g cornflour
½ pint milk	250ml milk
¼ pint single cream	125ml single cream
grated nutmeg	grated nutmeg
parsley, chopped	parsley, chopped

Serves six to eight
Preparation time: 15 minutes (plus 10 minutes for stock)
Cooking time: 40 minutes (plus 2 hours for stock)

Put carcass, bouquet garni and 4 oz (100g) of the onion into a large pan. Cover with water and bring to boil, then simmer for about 2 hours. Strain and cool. Remove any fat. Melt margarine, add vegetables and "sweat" them for 5-10 minutes, stirring from time to time. Add turkey stock, salt and pepper to taste, and the bay leaves. Bring to boil then simmer for about 30 minutes. Remove bay leaves. Blend cornflour with milk and add to pan. Bring to boil and boil for 2 minutes, stirring all the time. Add cream and stir through soup without allowing it to boil again. Add nutmeg, check and adjust seasoning if necessary. Sprinkle a little parsley on top and serve.

Above centre: Duck Soup
Left: Cucumber Soup
Right: Turkey Soup

CHICKEN LIVER PATE

Imperial	Metric
3oz butter	75g butter
1 small clove garlic or pinch garlic salt	1 small clove garlic or pinch garlic salt
4 rashers unsmoked streaky bacon, chopped	4 rashers unsmoked streaky bacon, chopped
1 small onion or 2oz mushrooms, chopped	1 small onion or 50g mushrooms, chopped
pinch celery salt or thyme	pinch celery salt or thyme
8oz chicken livers, chopped	225g chicken livers, chopped
1 tablespoon cream	1 tablespoon cream
salt	salt
pepper	pepper
small pinch mixed spice	small pinch mixed spice
1 tablespoon sherry or brandy	1 tablespoon sherry or brandy

Serves four to six
Preparation time: 30 minutes
Cooking time: 30 minutes

Melt 2oz (50g) butter in pan, add chopped or crushed garlic, chopped bacon and onion or mushroom. Cook until soft. Add chopped livers, season and cook gently for about 5 minutes. Allow to cool, add cream and sherry or brandy. Pass twice through mincer or liquidizer. Turn into serving dish — smooth surface and cover with remaining 1oz (15g) melted butter. Chill. Serve with thin hot toast and butter.

CHICKEN WITH AVOCADO

Imperial	Metric
4 avocado pears	4 avocado pears
6oz cooked chicken breast	150g cooked chicken breast
1/2 red pepper	1/2 red pepper
salt	salt
lemon juice	lemon juice
mayonnaise	mayonnaise
stuffed olives	stuffed olives

Serves eight
Preparation time: 15 minutes

Halve and stone pears. Cut one thin slice pepper. Dice or mince the chicken, blend with a little mayonnaise, add salt to taste and a squeeze of lemon. Chop the red pepper finely and mix into the chicken. Pile the mixture into the hollow of the pear and garnish with a thin slice of red pepper and a slice of stuffed olive.

STUFFED APPLES

Imperial	Metric
8oz cooked chicken	225g cooked chicken
5fl oz natural yoghurt	125ml natural yoghurt
small carton cottage cheese	small carton cottage cheese
2oz pineapple chunks (optional)	50g pineapple chunks (optional)
2oz white grapes, peeled and pips removed	50g white grapes, peeled and pips removed
2 celery stalks, chopped	2 celery stalks, chopped
4 large apples	4 large apples
1oz almonds cut into slivers	25g almonds cut into slivers
grated rind of 1/2 lemon	grated rind of 1/2 lemon

Serves four
Preparation time: 30 minutes

Cut the chicken into small pieces and mix it with the drained pineapple, the peeled grapes and celery. Add the yoghurt and cottage cheese; mix well. Polish the apples and cut them in half, scoop out the flesh with a grapefruit knife or spoon. Remove the core and chop the rest of the apple flesh, adding it to the chicken mixture. Add a little salt and ground black pepper and then pile the mixture into the apple skins, 2 halves per person. Sprinkle the tops with the almonds and grated lemon rind. Serve with lettuce, tomato and crispbreads.

CHICKEN CREAM MOUSSE

Imperial	Metric
1 tablespoon gelatine	1 tablespoon gelatine
1/2 pint chicken stock	250ml chicken stock
8oz cooked chicken, finely diced or minced	225g cooked chicken, finely diced or minced
2 tablespoons lemon juice	2 tablespoons lemon juice
1 teaspoon celery salt	1 teaspoon celery salt
white pepper	white pepper
1/4 pint double cream	125ml double cream
1/4 pint mayonnaise	125ml mayonnaise

Serves eight
Preparation time: 20 minutes

Dissolve the gelatine in the stock, taking care not to boil. When cooled, stir in the chicken meat, lemon juice, flavourings and finally the mayonnaise. Whip the cream, and fold it into the mixture directly setting point has been reached. Pour into rinsed mould and leave to set. Serve with a colourful salad of lettuce, tomatoes, beet and green peppers.

Left: Chicken Liver Pate
Centre: Chicken with Avocado and Stuffed Apples
Right: Chicken Cream Mousse

CHICKEN LIVER TERRINE

Imperial	Metric
1lb chicken livers, chopped	450g chicken livers, chopped
4 tablespoons port or sherry	4 tablespoons port or sherry
8oz raw boiling bacon, finely chopped (shoulder cut)	225g raw boiling bacon, finely chopped (shoulder cut)
2oz mushrooms, finely chopped	50g mushrooms, finely chopped
12oz pork sausagemeat	350g pork sausagemeat
4 tablespoons dry white wine	4 tablespoons dry white wine
salt	salt
freshly ground black pepper	freshly ground black pepper
8oz streaky bacon to line the terrine or dish	225g streaky bacon to line the terrine or dish
1 small onion, finely chopped	1 small onion, finely chopped

Serves eight
Preparation time: 1 hour 20 minutes
Cooking time: 2 — 2 hours 30 minutes
Oven: 350°F, 180°C, Gas Mark 4

Wash the livers, pat dry with kitchen paper and put into a basin with the port or sherry and leave to marinate for at least an hour. Mix the bacon, mushrooms and sausagemeat, stir in the port or sherry from the marinade and add the white wine. Add the salt and ground black pepper. Add the chopped liver and mix thoroughly. Line a 2 pint (1.2 litre) dish with ¾ of bacon, put in layers of the mixture and the chopped livers ending with a layer of mixture. Cover with more strips of streaky bacon then cover with foil. Stand dish in a baking tin with hot water to reach halfway up the dish and cook in centre of oven 350°F, (180°C, Gas Mark 4) for 2-2½ hours. Allow to cool then store in refrigerator.

CHICKEN PANCAKES

Imperial	Metric
1oz butter or margarine	25g butter or margarine
1 small onion, finely chopped	1 small onion, finely chopped
1oz flour	25g flour
½ pint milk	250ml milk
salt	salt
pepper	pepper
pinch of mixed herbs	pinch of mixed herbs
2-3oz mushrooms, sliced thinly	50-75g mushrooms, sliced thinly
8oz cooked chicken, cubed	200g cooked chicken, cubed
4 pancakes made and kept warm	4 pancakes made and kept warm
1 tablespoon chopped parsley	1 tablespoon chopped parsley

Serves four
Preparation time: 20 to 25 minutes

Heat butter or margarine and fry onion gently without browning. Add the flour and cook for one minute. Gradually add the milk and cook for 2-3 minutes, stirring all the time. Add salt and pepper, the mixed herbs and the sliced mushrooms and simmer for 5-10 minutes. Stir in the cubed chicken and heat through. Put a quarter of the filling onto each pancake, shape into a fan and serve at once, sprinkled with a little chopped parsley over each. **N.B.** The pancakes and the filling can be made in advance and then heated and assembled just before serving.

MORCOTT EGGS WITH CHICKEN

Imperial	Metric
4oz cooked chicken, finely chopped	100g cooked chicken, finely chopped
4 large eggs, hardboiled and halved	4 large eggs, hardboiled and halved
1 small clove garlic, crushed	1 small clove garlic, crushed
pinch of dried tarragon	pinch of dried tarragon
salt	salt
pepper	pepper
2 tablespoons single cream	2 tablespoons single cream
4 very thin slices cooked ham	4 very thin slices cooked ham
Sauce	**Sauce**
½ pint thick coating white sauce	250ml thick coating white sauce
2 tablespoons white wine	2 tablespoons white wine
2oz grated cheese	50g grated cheese
Topping	**Topping**
1 tablespoon grated cheese	1 tablespoon grated cheese
1 tablespoon breadcrumbs	1 tablespoon breadcrumbs
Garnish	**Garnish**
2-3oz small button mushrooms, cooked whole in butter	50-75g small button mushrooms, cooked whole in butter
parsley sprigs	parsley sprigs

Serves four
Preparation time: 30 minutes
Cooking time: 5 to 10 minutes

Grease 4 small ovenproof dishes. Mix together the chicken, garlic, tarragon, salt and pepper. Scoop out and add yolks. Bind with the cream. Pack the mixture back into 4 of the egg white halves and fit the other halves back on to them. If there is any chicken mixture left, put some in the base of each dish. Wrap a slice of ham around each egg and place one in each dish. Reheat the sauce and stir in the wine and cheese. Divide the cheese and wine sauce between the dishes, sprinkle with cheese and breadcrumbs and grill until golden brown. Put some mushrooms and a sprig of parsley on top of each dish and serve.

N.B. If preferred, one larger dish can be used, as shown above.

Left: Chicken Pancakes
Above right: Morcott Eggs with Chicken
Below right: Chicken Liver Terrine

BRANDIED CHICKEN TERRINE

Imperial	Metric
3½lb chicken	1.5kg chicken
4 tablespoons brandy	4 tablespoons brandy
1lb fresh belly of pork	400g fresh belly of pork
2 medium onions, peeled	2 medium onions, peeled
2 cloves garlic, peeled	2 cloves garlic, peeled
2 eggs, beaten	2 eggs, beaten
4oz mushrooms, chopped	100g mushrooms, chopped
6oz streaky bacon, rind removed	150g streaky bacon, rind removed
salt	salt
pepper	pepper

Serves seven to eight
Preparation time: 1 hour 30 minutes
Cooking time: 2 hours
Oven: 325°F, 160°C, Gas Mark 3

Remove skin from chicken and with a sharp knife take off the breast meat. Cut into ¼-inch (0.5cm) strips and put in brandy to marinate for at least an hour. Turn the meat over from time to time. Remove the remaining meat from the chicken and mince it coarsely with the belly of pork, the onions and garlic. Add the eggs and mushrooms, the brandy marinade, salt and pepper. Mix thoroughly. Line a 2-pint (1.2 litres) pie dish with ¾ of the streaky bacon. Put in alternate layers of minced meats and the chicken strips, ending with the minced meats. Top with strips of streaky bacon and cover closely with foil. Stand dish in a baking tin with hot water to reach halfway up the dish. Cook at 325°F (160°C, Gas Mark 3) for about 2 hours. Allow to cool then store in the refrigerator.

Above: Chicken Creams
Below: Brandied Chicken Terrine

26

CHICKEN CREAMS

Imperial	Metric
8oz raw chicken breast meat	200g raw chicken breast meat
2 eggs	2 eggs
salt	salt
pepper	pepper
pinch of ground mace	pinch of ground mace
1/2 pint cream	250ml cream
Sauce	**Sauce**
1oz butter	25g butter
1oz flour	25g flour
1/4 pint chicken stock	125ml chicken stock
1/4 pint dry white wine	125ml dry white wine
salt	salt
pepper	pepper
2oz button mushrooms, sliced	50g button mushrooms, sliced
4 tablespoons cream	4 tablespoons cream
chopped parsley	chopped parsley

Serves six
Preparation time: 25 minutes
Cooking time: 30 minutes
Oven: 400°F, 200°C, Gas Mark 6

First mince the chicken meat, then liquidize with the eggs and seasonings. Pour into a bowl and gradually whisk in the cream. Lightly oil some small individual oven-proof moulds. Pour the chicken mixture into them and stand them in a baking tin which is half filled with hot water. Bake in oven 400°F (200°C, Gas Mark 6) for about 30 minutes until set.

Sauce: Make sauce by melting butter, then stir in flour and cook for 1-2 minutes; gradually add stock and wine and seasoning. Heat until thickened, stirring all the time. Add the mushrooms and simmer for 2-3 minutes. Add the cream and chopped parsley. Turn the moulds out on to a hot serving dish. Pour the sauce over them and serve at once, accompanied by crusty bread or rolls.

POTTED TURKEY

Imperial	Metric
12oz cooked turkey meat	350g cooked turkey meat
3oz butter	75g butter
3oz cooked ham or boiling bacon	75g cooked ham or boiling bacon
salt	salt
pepper	pepper
1 small onion, chopped and cooked, without browning, in a little butter	1 small onion, chopped and cooked, without browning, in a little butter

Serves four to six
Preparation time: 15 minutes

Finely mince the turkey meat, ham and cooked onion or blend in an electric blender. Add 2oz (50g) of the butter, and the seasoning, then mix thoroughly. Turn into a bowl and pour the remaining 1oz (25g) butter, melted, over the top and chill.

DUCK PATE

Imperial	Metric
2 ducks	2 ducks
1½lb minced fat pork	700g minced fat pork
4oz pork, cubed	113g pork, cubed
¼ pint white wine	125ml white wine
2 tablespoons brandy	2 tablespoons brandy
6 peppercorns	6 peppercorns
6 juniper berries, crushed	6 juniper berries, crushed
2 garlic cloves, crushed	2 garlic cloves, crushed
salt	salt
black pepper	black pepper
marjoram	marjoram
cayenne	cayenne
unsmoked streaky bacon or fat pork	unsmoked streaky bacon or fat pork

Serves six to eight
Preparation time: 45 minutes
Cooking time: 1 hour 30 minutes
             (plus one hour initial cooking)
Oven: 350°F, 180°C, Gas Mark 4, then
      300°F, 150°C, Gas Mark 2

Roast ducks at 350°F (180°C, Gas Mark 4) for 1 hour. Allow to cool. Take meat off the bones, discard the skin and keep the juices. Chop or mince meat coarsely, mix with minced and cubed pork. Blend in duck juices, wine, brandy, peppercorns, juniper berries, crushed garlic, salt and pepper, marjoram and cayenne. Line mould with slices of fat pork or bacon and press in the mixture. Cover with cooking foil and cook in a bain-marie at 300°F (150°C, Gas Mark 2) for 1½ hours. Chill pâté well and turn out.

DUCK AND ORANGE TERRINE

Imperial	Metric
1 small duck	1 small duck
3-4 tablespoons brandy	3-4 tablespoons brandy
12oz fresh belly of pork	350g fresh belly of pork
1 onion, medium size, peeled	1 onion, medium size, peeled
rind of 1 orange, cut into very thin slices	rind of 1 orange, cut into very thin slices
1 large or 2 small eggs, beaten	1 large or 2 small eggs, beaten
pinch of dried thyme	pinch of dried thyme
salt	salt
pepper	pepper
8oz streaky bacon	225g streaky bacon
Garnish	**Garnish**
orange slices	orange slices

Serves six to eight
Preparation time: 3 hours 30 minutes
Cooking time: 2 hours
Oven: 350°F, 180°C, Gas Mark 4

Slice the breast meat off the bird and cut into thin strips. Put these to marinate in the brandy for 2-3 hours. Take off the remaining meat from the bird. Mince the duck meat with the pork and onion, add the orange rind, eggs, brandy from the marinade, the thyme, salt and pepper. Line a 1½ pint (900ml) dish with ¾ of the streaky bacon and put in alternating layers of minced meat and the marinated strips of breast meat, finishing with the minced meat. Put remaining strips of streaky bacon over top and cover with foil. Stand dish in a baking tin which is half filled with hot water, and cook in moderate oven at 350°F (180°C, Gas Mark 4) for about 2 hours. Cool, then put in refrigerator. Garnish with slices of orange.

Left: Duck and Orange Terrine
Above right: Duck Pate
Below right: Potted Turkey

Main Meals

CURRIED CHICKEN WITH RICE

Imperial	Metric
1oz butter	25g butter
3 chicken quarters	3 chicken quarters
½lb onion, peeled and chopped	225g onion, peeled and chopped
2 cloves garlic, very finely chopped (optional)	2 cloves garlic, very finely chopped (optional)
1 tablespoon flour	1 tablespoon flour
1½-2 tablespoons curry powder	1½-2 tablespoons curry powder
1 pint chicken stock	575ml chicken stock
1 apple, peeled and cored	1 apple, peeled and cored
4oz sultanas	100g sultanas
salt	salt
pepper	pepper
6oz rice	150g rice
Garnish	**Garnish**
3 pineapple rings	3 pineapple rings
cranberry sauce	cranberry sauce

Serves three
Preparation time: 25 minutes
Cooking time: 1 hour

Melt the butter in a large heavy saucepan or casserole and fry the chicken quarters in it until lightly brown all over. Remove from the fat and keep hot. Fry the chopped onion and the garlic, if used, until golden brown and then stir in the flour and curry powder. Cook gently for 1 minute. Add the stock slowly, stirring well and then add the chopped apple, sultanas and seasoning. Stir. Add the chicken quarters, bring to the boil, cover the pan and simmer for about 1 hour or until the meat is tender, stirring occasionally to prevent sticking. Cook the rice and serve with the curry. Garnish each portion with a hot pineapple ring with a little cranberry sauce in the centre of each ring.

SPRING CHICKEN EN COCOTTE

Imperial	Metric
a little flour	a little flour
salt	salt
pepper	pepper
2oz butter	50g butter
3lb chicken	1.5kg chicken
12 button mushrooms	12 button mushrooms
12 pickling onions, peeled and left whole	12 pickling onions, peeled and left whole
¼ pint white wine	150ml white wine
4-8 tomatoes	4-8 tomatoes

Serves four
Preparation time: 15 minutes
Cooking time: 1 hour
Oven: 400°F, 200°C, Gas Mark 6

Season the flour well and dust the chicken with it. Heat the butter in a casserole and turn the chicken round in it until coated all over. Add the mushrooms, onions and wine to the casserole. Cover and cook for 45 minutes at 400°F (200°C, Gas Mark 6). Then add the tomatoes and cook for a further 15 minutes without the lid. Serve with the liquid and vegetables round the chicken.

Above left: Spring Chicken en Cocotte
Below left: Curried Chicken with Rice
Right: Winter Casserole

WINTER CASSEROLE

Imperial	Metric
3¼lb chicken, jointed into 8 and skinned	1.5kg chicken, jointed into 8 and skinned
1¼oz butter	30g butter
1 large onion, peeled and sliced into rings	1 large onion, peeled and sliced into rings
½lb swede, peeled and diced	225g swede, peeled and diced
½lb carrots, diced or sliced	225g carrots, diced or sliced
1 tablespoon flour	1 tablespoon flour
½ teaspoon marjoram	½ teaspoon marjoram
1 level teaspoon salt	1 level teaspoon salt
pepper	pepper
½ pint chicken stock	275ml chicken stock

Serves four
Preparation time: 25 minutes
Cooking time: 1 hour 15 minutes
Oven: 350°F, 180°C, Gas Mark 4

Skin the joints by holding the skin with a piece of kitchen paper or piece of cloth and pulling firmly. Melt the butter and fry the joints for a few minutes until they are turning brown on all sides. Remove the portions and place in a casserole. Keep them warm. Add the onion to the pan and cook gently until beginning to soften, then add the remaining vegetables, turning them in the fat. Fry all the vegetables together for about 5 minutes. Sprinkle the flour over the vegetables and stir it in well. Transfer the vegetable mixture to the casserole with the chicken, sprinkle the marjoram over, add the seasoning and pour on the stock. Cook for 1¼ hours at 350°F (180°C, Gas Mark 4).

SPRING CHICKEN AND EGG SAUCE

Imperial	Metric
3½lb chicken	1.6kg chicken
1 small onion stuck with 4 cloves	1 small onion stuck with 4 cloves
½ teaspoon each of chopped basil and tarragon	½ teaspoon each of chopped basil and tarragon
sprig of parsley	sprig of parsley
pinch of mace	pinch of mace
salt	salt
pepper	pepper
¼ pint chicken stock	150ml chicken stock
4 tablespoons white wine	4 tablespoons white wine
2 egg yolks	2 egg yolks
1oz butter	25g butter
1 hardboiled egg	1 hardboiled egg
1 teaspoon chopped parsley	1 teaspoon chopped parsley
Garnish	**Garnish**
1 hardboiled egg	1 hardboiled egg
chopped parsley	chopped parsley

Serves four
Preparation time: 15 minutes
Cooking time: 1 hour 10 minutes

Place the onion with cloves, herbs and mace inside the bird with a sprinkling of salt and pepper. Heat the stock and wine in a heavy saucepan with a lid. Put the bird into the pan and put on the lid which must be tight fitting. Put a piece of greaseproof paper inside if it is not. Simmer very gently for approximately 1 hour or until tender. Drain the chicken and remove the skin and the onion from inside; keep the bird hot. Add a little of the cooking liquor to the egg yolks and then blend this back into the rest of the liquor together with the butter in small pieces. Heat this sauce very gently, stirring all the time until it thickens, but be very careful not to let it boil. Add the chopped hardboiled egg and parsley and season to taste with salt and pepper. Pour the sauce over the bird and garnish with sieved hardboiled egg and finely chopped parsley.

CRUNCHY BRAN CHICKEN

Imperial	Metric
4 chicken quarters	4 chicken quarters
seasoned flour for coating	seasoned flour for coating
1 egg	1 egg
4 teaspoons Dijon mustard	4 teaspoons Dijon mustard
3oz bran flakes	75g bran flakes
3 tablespoons grated cheese	3 tablespoons grated cheese
a little vegetable oil	a little vegetable oil

Serves four
Preparation time: 25 minutes
Cooking time: 1 hour
Oven: 375°F, 190°C, Gas Mark 5

Wipe and dry quarters. Skin them, if preferred. Toss in the seasoned flour. Beat egg and blend in the mustard. Crush bran flakes with a rolling pin, add cheese and put on to a piece of greaseproof paper or a plate. Brush quarters carefully with egg and mustard, then coat with the flakes and cheese mixture. Press on firmly. Leave to harden slightly for 5 minutes. Place joints on baking dish or tin and sprinkle a little oil over them. Bake at 375°F (190°C, Gas Mark 5) for about 1 hour or until tender. Drain on kitchen paper then serve very hot. Accompany by a tossed mixed salad for summer or try a winter salad of diced apples, celery, beetroot and onions with walnuts and raisins in either a light French or yoghurt dressing.

Left: Crunchy Bran Chicken
Centre: Spring Chicken and Egg Sauce
Right: Chicken with Sesame Seeds

CHICKEN WITH SESAME SEEDS

Imperial	Metric
4 chicken breasts	4 chicken breasts
3oz plain flour	75g plain flour
salt	salt
pepper	pepper
1 tablespoon sesame seeds	1 tablespoon sesame seeds
½ tablespoon ground coriander	½ tablespoon ground coriander
1 teaspoon ground ginger	1 teaspoon ground ginger
pinch chilli powder	pinch chilli powder
3oz butter	75g butter
1 tablespoon olive oil	1 tablespoon olive oil
½ pint chicken stock	275ml chicken stock
3 tablespoons dry white wine	3 tablespoons dry white wine
1 tablespoon chopped parsley	1 tablespoon chopped parsley
1 tablespoon chopped watercress	1 tablespoon chopped watercress
2 sprigs fresh rosemary, stripped	2 sprigs fresh rosemary, stripped
1 pint double cream	600ml double cream
6oz long-grain rice	175g long-grain rice
1 tablespoon melted butter	1 tablespoon melted butter

Serves four
Preparation time: 15 minutes

Season the flour with the salt, pepper, sesame seeds, coriander, ginger and chilli powder. Coat the chicken portions evenly. Fry the chicken portions in the butter and olive oil for 10 minutes on each side. Transfer the chicken to a warm dish and keep hot. Stir the remaining seasoned flour into the frying pan; add the chicken stock, rosemary and wine. Bring to the boil, simmer gently for 20 minutes, or until reduced by half. Add remaining chopped herbs to sauce. Stir in the cream and reheat gently. Cook the rice in boiling salted water for 12 minutes. Drain and rinse with hot water. Stir in the melted butter. Pile the rice into a serving dish and arrange the chicken portions on top. Serve the sauce in a sauceboat.

CHICKEN TIMBALE

Imperial	Metric
8-12oz chicken meat, chopped	225-350g chicken meat, chopped
3oz butter	75g butter
2½oz flour	65g flour
8fl oz milk flavoured with onions and herbs	200ml milk flavoured with onions and herbs
2 eggs	2 eggs
3-4 tablespoons double cream	3-4 tablespoons double cream
16-20 mushrooms, quartered	16-20 mushrooms, quartered
½-¾ pint well-flavoured brown stock	250-425ml well-flavoured brown stock
1 tablespoon herbs, chopped	1 tablespoon herbs, chopped
2 teaspoons Worcester sauce	2 teaspoons Worcester sauce
2-3 tablespoons Madeira or sherry	2-3 tablespoons Madeira or sherry

Serves four
Preparation time: 30 minutes
Cooking time: 35 minutes
Oven: 350°F, 180°C, Gas Mark 4

Pre-heat oven to 350°F (180°C, Gas Mark 4). Melt 1oz (25g) butter, stir in 1oz (25g) flour. Heat the milk. Pour in to roux and bring to the boil, stirring constantly. Cook for a few minutes, add seasoning and leave to cool. Mince chicken finely in blender and mix with eggs beaten in cream. Add cooled sauce. Mix together and turn into a thoroughly buttered ring mould, allowing a little space at the top for expansion while cooking. Cover with buttered paper. Put in roasting pan of hot water and bake for 25-35 minutes or until a skewer can be inserted into the centre and come out clean. Run a knife around the outside and inner ring of mould, and turn out onto a larger round plate. While the timbale cooks, make mushroom sauce: Melt remaining 1½oz (35g) butter and cook quartered mushrooms for 2-3 minutes. Then sprinkle in 1½oz (35g) flour. Cook for 1 minute, remove from heat and add brown, well-flavoured stock and blend thoroughly. Bring to the boil and simmer for a few minutes. Add seasoning, herbs and Worcester sauce, and Madeira or sherry. Allow flavours to blend well before pouring into centre of mould.

SPRING CHICKEN IN MUSHROOM SAUCE

Imperial	Metric
2½lb chicken	1.1kg chicken
1oz flour	25g flour
salt	salt
pepper	pepper
2oz butter	50g butter
8oz small mushrooms	225g small mushrooms
½-¾ pint milk	250-425ml milk
2 tablespoons Burgundy or port	2 tablespoons Burgundy or port
Garnish	**Garnish**
paprika	paprika
chopped parsley	chopped parsley

Serves three
Preparation time: 30 minutes
Cooking time: 1 hour
Oven: 375°F, 190°C, Gas Mark 5

Cut the chicken in half, along the breast and backbone. Season 1 teaspoon of the flour and sprinkle the chicken with this. Heat the butter in a frying pan and turn the chicken in it until the flour coating is pale brown. Put bird in a casserole. Chop half the mushrooms and toss these in the remaining butter. Add the rest of the flour stir well and cook gently for 1 minute, then slowly add the milk stirring all the time. When smooth, bring slowly to the boil and cook until the sauce has thickened, stirring all the time. Season well and then stir in the Burgundy or port and pour over the chicken. Arrange the rest of the whole mushrooms around the chicken. Put a lid on the casserole and cook for 50-60 minutes in the centre of an oven at 375°F (190°C, Gas Mark 5). Serve from the casserole. Garnish helpings with paprika and chopped parsley.

Above: Spring Chicken in Mushroom Sauce
Below: Chicken Timbale

MACARONI CHICKEN

Imperial	Metric
4 chicken quarters	4 chicken quarters
1 small onion, peeled	1 small onion, peeled
bouquet garni or	bouquet garni or
1 teaspoon mixed herbs	1 teaspoon mixed herbs
1½ chicken stock cubes	1½ chicken stock cubes
1 pint water	575ml water
6oz macaroni	150g macaroni
½ pint milk	250ml milk
¾oz flour	20g flour
1oz butter	25g butter
1 egg yolk	1 egg yolk
salt	salt
pepper	pepper

Serves four
Preparation time: 10 minutes
Cooking time: 1 hour 45 minutes

Place the quarters, whole onion, bouquet garni or herbs and crumbled stock cubes into an iron casserole or large saucepan with a lid and pour in the water. Bring to the boil and then simmer with a lid on for 45 minutes. Then, wearing rubber gloves remove the meat carefully from the bones and discard the bones and skin but retain the cooking liquor. Take ¾ pint (425ml) of the cooking liquor and make it up to 1 pint (575ml) with water. Use this to cook the macaroni. Bring to the boil and simmer for 12-15 minutes or until tender. Meanwhile, add the milk to the remaining stock, put the chicken back into this and simmer for a further 15 minutes. Then remove the chicken and keep it hot. Blend the butter and flour together until a smooth paste is formed and add this, a little at a time, to the hot milk and stock, stirring all the time. Beat the egg yolk and add this to the sauce. Stir the sauce over a gentle heat until it thickens and season well. Drain the noodles, place the chicken on top and pour the sauce over.

CHICKEN BOURGUIGNON

Imperial	Metric
6lb chicken	2.75kg chicken
with giblets	with giblets
1 teaspoon fresh	1 teaspoon fresh
chopped herbs	chopped herbs
½ teaspoon mixed spice	½ teaspoon mixed spice
salt	salt
freshly ground black	freshly ground black
pepper	pepper
8oz streaky bacon	225g streaky bacon
6 shallots or 2 medium	6 shallots or 2 medium
onions, quartered	onions, quartered
8oz button mushrooms	225g button mushrooms
½ bottle red wine	½ bottle red wine
1oz butter	25g butter
2 teaspoons cornflour	2 teaspoons cornflour

Serves eight
Preparation time: 35 minutes
Cooking time: 3 hours 15 minutes to 3 hours 45 minutes
Oven: 325°F, 160°C, Gas Mark 3

Sprinkle the inside of the chicken with the herbs, spice and seasoning, but do not stuff. Cover the breast with overlapping bacon rashers and place in a large baking tin. Chop the chicken liver and heart and put into a saucepan with the onions, mushroom stalks and wine. Simmer gently for 15 minutes and then remove the onions. Keep onions warm. Pour the wine and mushroom stalks over the chicken and then cook it in the oven 325°F (160°C, Gas Mark 3) for 3-3½ hours, basting frequently with the liquid. Thirty minutes before the end of the cooking time remove the bacon, add the mushrooms and onions to the baking tin and continue to baste frequently. When the chicken is cooked, place it on a warm serving dish and put the mushrooms and onions around it. Keep warm. Pour the wine mixture back into a saucepan, add the butter to it and thicken with the cornflour blended with a little water. Boil until thickened, adjust the seasoning and serve with the chicken.

Above: Macaroni Chicken
Below: Chicken Bourguignon

OLD ENGLISH ROAST CHICKEN

Stuff the chicken as usual and place strips of bacon across the breast. Roast with a few bacon rolls. Make a thick gravy using the giblets and add a little stout or brown ale. From a packet mix, make as many tiny, light stuffing balls as bacon rolls, and place them alternately around the chicken about ½ an hour before the chicken is ready. Garnish with watercress and serve with jacket potatoes.

Serves four
Preparation time: 10 minutes
Cooking time: according to size of bird used
Oven: 375°F, 190°C, Gas Mark 5

ECONOMICAL CASSEROLE

Imperial	Metric
½lb leeks	225g leeks
½lb carrots	225g carrots
3lb chicken, cut into quarters or 4 chicken quarters	1.5kg chicken, cut into quarters or 4 chicken quarters
1½oz flour	35g flour
1oz butter	25g butter
1 tablespoon oil	1 tablespoon oil
1 pint chicken stock	575ml chicken stock
1 bay leaf	1 bay leaf
salt	salt
pepper	pepper
½lb potatoes	225g potatoes

Serves four
Preparation time: 40 minutes
Cooking time: 1 hour 30 minutes
Oven: 350°F, 180°C, Gas Mark 4

Wash and slice the leeks and the carrots. Coat the chicken quarters well in the flour. Heat the butter and oil and fry the chicken until browned all over. Remove the chicken and place in a large casserole. Fry the leeks and carrots in the fat until they begin to soften; add any remaining flour, stir well and add to the casserole. Pour in the stock, add the bay leaf and season well with salt and pepper. Cook for 35 minutes at 350°F (180°C, Gas Mark 4). Meanwhile, peel and dice the potatoes and add to the casserole after 35 minutes. Return to the oven for a further 50 minutes or until the chicken and vegetables are well cooked and tender.

CHICKEN MIMOSA

Imperial	Metric
3lb chicken, cut into quarters or 4 chicken quarters	1.5kg chicken, cut into quarters or 4 chicken quarters
1oz butter	25g butter
1oz flour	25g flour
1 pint milk	575ml milk
½ teaspoon tarragon	½ teaspoon tarragon
salt	salt
pepper	pepper
1 tablespoon lemon juice	1 tablespoon lemon juice
2 tablespoons double cream	2 tablespoons double cream
2 eggs	2 eggs
Garnish	**Garnish**
parsley	parsley

Serves three to four
Preparation time: 20 minutes
Cooking time: 1 hour 30 minutes

Melt the butter, add the flour and then slowly add the milk to make a white sauce. Bring to the boil, stirring well and then add the tarragon and chicken. Season. Simmer gently in a covered pan for about an hour or until the chicken is tender; stir from time to time to prevent sticking. Meanwhile, hardboil one of the eggs and then separate the yolk from the white and chop the white finely. Beat the other egg and add the cream. When the chicken is cooked, remove it from the sauce and take the meat off the bone. Keep hot. Strain the sauce to remove any pieces of bone which may have cooked into it. Then add the egg/cream mixture together with the lemon juice and the chopped egg white. Season and then reheat the sauce gently but do not boil. Pour the sauce over the chicken meat and sprinkle the top with the remaining egg yolk, sieved. Garnish with a little parsley.

Above left: Economical Casserole
Above right: Chicken Mimosa
Centre: Old English Roast Chicken

HERBED SPRING CHICKEN

Imperial	Metric
2½lb chicken, approx	1kg chicken, approx
½ teaspoon rosemary	½ teaspoon rosemary
½ teaspoon oregano	½ teaspoon oregano
½ teaspoon marjoram	½ teaspoon marjoram
1oz butter	25g butter
1-2 tablespoon lemon juice	1-2 tablespoon lemon juice
4fl. oz. white wine	125ml white wine
1 teaspoon cornflour	1 teaspoon cornflour
1 tablespoon double cream	1 tablespoon double cream
salt	salt
pepper	pepper

Serves three to four
Preparation time: 15 minutes
Cooking time: 60 minutes
Oven: 375°F, 190°C, Gas Mark 5

Cut the chicken into 8 portions and remove the skin, by holding it with a cloth or piece of kitchen paper and pulling firmly. Lay the portions of chicken on a plate and sprinkle them with the herbs and seasoning. Melt the butter in frying pan and brown the chicken portions all over. Place the portions in a casserole. Mix together the wine and lemon juice, add to the juices in the pan, bring to the boil and pour over the chicken. Cover and cook for 50 minutes at 375°F, (190°C, Gas Mark 5). Meanwhile, blend the cornflour with a little water to a smooth cream. When the chicken is cooked drain it and place in a serving dish. Add the cornflour mixture to the juices from the casserole, bring to the boil and simmer until thickened. Stir in the cream, adjust the seasoning and pour over the chicken.

CHICKEN GOULASH

Imperial	Metric
3½lb chicken	1.5kg chicken
1 large onion	1 large onion
1½oz fat	35g fat
1oz flour	25g flour
¾ pint chicken stock	425ml chicken stock
2 tablespoons tomato purée	2 tablespoons tomato purée
1 level teaspoon paprika	1 level teaspoon paprika
salt	salt
freshly ground black pepper	freshly ground black pepper
1 tablespoon soured cream	1 tablespoon soured cream

Serves four
Preparation time: 20 minutes
Cooking times: 1 hour 15 minutes
Oven: 325°F, 160°C, Gas Mark 3

Peel and slice the onion. Joint the chicken into 8 portions (2 breast, 2 thigh, 2 drumsticks, 2 wings) and remove the skin. Heat the fat and fry the joints in it, turning frequently, until brown all over. Place them in a casserole. Fry the sliced onion in the remaining fat until soft and then spread it over the chicken in the casserole. Stir the flour into the fat in the pan and cook gently, stirring until it turns brown. Add the stock very slowly, stirring until smooth and then add the purée, paprika, salt and black pepper. Bring to the boil, stirring well and then pour over the chicken in the casserole. Cover and cook for 1¼ hours at 325°F (160°C, Gas Mark 3) or until the chicken is tender. Stir in the soured cream before serving.

POT ROASTED CHICKEN

Imperial	Metric
½ pint strong chicken stock—made with giblets	250ml strong chicken stock—made with giblets
3¼lb roasting chicken	1.4kg roasting chicken
salt	salt
ground black pepper	ground black pepper
2oz butter or dripping	50g butter or dripping
8oz carrots, scraped and cut into 1½" pieces	225g carrots, scraped and cut into 3.5cm pieces
8oz small onions or large onion cut into pieces	225g small onion or large onion cut into pieces
bouquet garni	bouquet garni
1lb small, even-sized potatoes, peeled	450g small, even-sized potatoes, peeled
½oz flour	15g flour

Serves four
Preparation time: 15 minutes
Cooking time: 75 minutes

For the stock remove the bird's giblets and put them in a pan, cover with water and season. Remove any fat from inside the bird. Heat the butter in a large heavy pan or metal casserole. Turn the chicken in it until it is golden brown all over. Add the carrots and the onion, fry, turning for 3-4 minutes and then pour over the stock. Season well with salt and freshly ground black pepper. Put in bouquet garni. Cover the pan with a tight fitting lid, turn the heat low and cook for 35 minutes, then add the potatoes; baste and cook for a further 30-35 minutes until the chicken is tender and the potatoes are soft. Remove the chicken to a hot serving dish and surround with the vegetables, reserving the liquid. Blend the flour with a little water until a smooth paste, add a little of the hot liquid from the pan and then stir the flour mixture back into the remaining liquid in the pan. Bring to the boil, simmer for 3 minutes and serve as gravy with the chicken and vegetables.

Left: Herbed Spring Chicken
Centre: Chicken Goulash
Right: Pot Roasted Chicken

CHICKEN CASSEROLE

Imperial	Metric
2½lb chicken	1.25kg chicken
½oz butter	15g butter
1 tablespoon oil	1 tablespoon oil
salt	salt
pepper	pepper
1 level teaspoon dried tarragon (fresh if available)	1 level teaspoon dried tarragon (fresh if available)
1 medium onion, peeled and sliced	1 medium onion, peeled and sliced
½oz flour	15g flour
8oz can tomatoes	226g can tomatoes
7oz can sweetcorn kernels	198g can sweetcorn kernels
4fl oz chicken stock	100ml chicken stock

Serves four
Preparation time: 20 minutes
Cooking time: 50 minutes
Oven: 350°F, 180°C, Gas Mark 4

Joint the chicken into 8 portions (2 breasts, 2 thighs, 2 wings, 2 drumsticks). Remove the skin by holding it firmly with a cloth or piece of kitchen paper and pulling it off the portion. Heat the butter and oil together and fry the joints in this until turning brown all over. Place the joints in a casserole and sprinkle them with salt, pepper and the tarragon. Fry the sliced onions in the remaining fat in the pan, gently until soft but not brown, then sprinkle the flour over and stir well until all the fat has been absorbed. Add the can of tomatoes with the juice, the drained sweetcorn and the stock. Stir well and bring to the boil, then pour over the chicken in the casserole. Cover the casserole and cook for about 1 hour at 350°F (180°C, Gas Mark 4) or until the chicken is really tender. Serve hot.

TASTY GRILLED CHICKEN

Imperial	Metric
2½lb chicken, jointed or 4 chicken quarters cut through at the ball and socket joints to make 8 portions	1.1kg chicken, jointed or 4 chicken quarters cut through at the ball and socket joints to make 8 portions
1 garlic clove, cut in half	1 garlic clove, cut in half
cooking oil	cooking oil
2 tablespoons lemon juice	2 tablespoons lemon juice
salt	salt
pepper	pepper
4oz mushrooms, peeled and thinly sliced	100g mushrooms, peeled and thinly sliced
4oz lean cooked ham, cut into fine strips	100g lean cooked ham, cut into fine strips
chopped parsley	chopped parsley

Serves four
Preparation time: 10 minutes
Cooking time: 45 minutes

Rub the base of the grill pan with cut side of garlic. Place the chicken in the pan and brush a little oil over each portion. Distribute lemon juice, salt and pepper evenly. Grill under a medium heat for 30-40 minutes, turning as necessary and keeping the portions well basted with the juices in the pan. When cooked, remove the portions from the grill pan and keep hot. Pour away all but about 2 tablespoons fat in the pan and add the mushrooms; grill for a few minutes until tender and then add the ham, mixing well with the mushrooms. Top the chicken portions with the mushroom and ham mixture and sprinkle with the chopped parsley. Serve hot with a crisp green salad.

STUFFED CHICKEN EN COCOTTE

Imperial	Metric
3-3½lb chicken	1.5kg chicken
salt	salt
pepper	pepper
2oz butter	50g butter
4oz lean bacon, cut into pieces	100g lean bacon, cut into pieces
1 medium onion, roughly chopped	1 medium onion, roughly chopped
1lb small, even-sized potatoes, peeled	450g small, even-sized potatoes, peeled
Stuffing	**Stuffing**
4oz pork sausagemeat	100g pork sausagemeat
1 heaped tablespoon fresh breadcrumbs	1 heaped tablespoon fresh breadcrumbs
1 tablespoon chopped parsley	1 tablespoon chopped parsley
liver from the chicken, chopped	liver from the chicken, chopped

Serves four to five
Preparation time: 25 minutes
Cooking time: 1 hour 30 minutes
Oven: 350°F, 180°C, Gas Mark 4

Remove the giblets from the chicken retaining the liver for the stuffing. Remove any fat from inside. Season. Mix together the ingredients for the stuffing and insert under the neck flap of the chicken. Secure the flap underneath with the wing tip. Melt the butter in a large heavy pan or iron casserole and lightly brown the chicken, turning it over frequently to ensure browning on all sides. Add the onion and the bacon, cover the pan and cook over a gentle heat for 15 minutes. Season well with salt and ground black pepper. If necessary, transfer to a casserole, baste the chicken and add the potatoes turning them in the fat. Cover with the lid and cook in a moderate oven 350°F (180°C, Gas Mark 4) for about 1½ hours. After about 1 hour, remove the lid and baste the chicken and potatoes and, if desired, leave the lid off to brown the potatoes a little. When the chicken is tender, place on a hot serving dish, surround with the potatoes, onion and bacon removed with a draining spoon. Skim any excess fat from the surface of the liquor and serve with the chicken. The dish can be sprinkled with chopped chives.

Above left: Chicken Casserole; Above right: Stuffed Chicken en Cocotte; Below Centre: Tasty Grilled Chicken

CHICKEN
A LA MOAMBE

Imperial	Metric
3lb chicken, cut into joints	1.3kg chicken, cut into joints
6 tablespoons oil	6 tablespoons oil
6oz tomato purée	150g tomato purée
¾ pint water	425ml water
1½ level teaspoons salt	1½ level teaspoons salt
½ teaspoon pepper	½ teaspoon pepper
3-4oz peanut butter	75-100g peanut butter

Serves four to six
Preparation time: 10 minutes
Cooking time: 30 minutes

Brown chicken pieces in hot oil in a large pan. Drain off surplus oil when chicken is browned. Combine tomato purée and water, and pour over chicken. Loosen chicken from pan and simmer for 10 minutes. Add salt, pepper and peanut butter, simmer for an additional 20 minutes.

Left: Chicken à la Moambe
Centre: Tandoori Murgha Baked Chicken
Right: Florida Chicken Casserole

TANDOORI MURGHA
BAKED CHICKEN

Imperial	Metric
3lb chicken	1.3kg chicken
4 tablespoons lemon juice	4 tablespoons lemon juice
½ teaspoon salt	½ teaspoon salt
1 tablespoon tandoori spice mixture	1 tablespoon tandoori spice mixture
1oz butter	25g butter

Serves four
Preparation time: (24 hours to marinate) 25 minutes
Cooking time: 45-55 minutes
Oven: 400°F, 200°C, Gas Mark 6

Wash and skin and thoroughly dry the chicken. Cut in halves lengthways. Make cuts ¼ inch (0.5cm) deep in the legs and breasts. Mix together 3 tablespoons lemon juice, salt and tandoori spice to make a paste. Rub the paste into the cuts. Leave for 24 hours in a cool place, Place in open baking tray breast up and add butter. Bake in oven 400°F (200°C, Gas Mark 6) for approximately 45-55 minutes or until tender, basting two or three times. Remove from oven. Sprinkle remaining lemon juice over the chicken and place under grill for a further 5 minutes. Serve immediately with fresh green salad.

FLORIDA CHICKEN CASSEROLE

Imperial	Metric
2½-3lb chicken	1.25-1.5kg chicken
1½oz flour	40g flour
1 teaspoon paprika	1 teaspoon paprika
1 teaspoon salt	1 teaspoon salt
ground black pepper	ground black pepper
1oz butter	25g butter
grated rind and juice of 1 orange	grated rind and juice of 1 orange
8oz can pineapple, chopped	226g can pineapple, chopped
1 large orange, sliced	1 large orange, sliced
4fl oz chicken stock	100ml chicken stock

Serves four
Preparation time: 25 minutes
Cooking time: 50 to 60 minutes
Oven: 350°F, 180°C, Gas Mark 4

Joint the chicken into 8 portions (2 breasts, 2 thighs, 2 drumsticks and 2 wings) and remove the skin by holding it firmly with a piece of cloth or kitchen paper and pulling the skin from the portions. Put the flour, paprika, salt and black pepper into a bag and shake the portions in this mixture until well coated. Heat the butter and fry the portions gently until really golden on all sides. Sprinkle the remaining flour mixture from the bag over the portions and turn them in the pan until the flour has absorbed all the butter in the pan and resembles fine breadcrumbs. Turn the chicken into a casserole. Sprinkle the chicken with the grated orange rind and pour the orange juice over. Place the chopped pineapple on top and pour over most of the juice from the can, and the chicken stock. Cover the casserole and cook for 50-60 minutes at 350°F (180°C, Gas Mark 4). 5 minutes before serving, arrange half-slices of orange around the chicken. Cook for a further 5 minutes without the lid. Serve with a green vegetable or green salad.

CRISPY NOODLES WITH CHICKEN AND VEGETABLES

Imperial	Metric
1lb Chinese dried egg noodles	450kg Chinese dried egg noodles
3 tablespoons oil	3 tablespoons oil
1½ tablespoon soy sauce	1½ tablespoon soy sauce
½ teaspoon sugar	½ teaspoon sugar
8oz cooked chicken, cut into strips	225g cooked chicken, cut into strips
3 spring onions, chopped	3 spring onions, chopped
1 inch piece fresh root ginger, thinly sliced	2.5cm piece fresh root ginger, thinly sliced
2½oz can bamboo shoots, cut into thin strips	65g can bamboo shoots, cut into thin strips
2 celery stalks, sliced	2 celery stalks, sliced
1 large carrot, sliced diagonally	1 large carrot, sliced diagonally
2oz mushrooms	50g mushrooms
1 teaspoon cornflour dissolved in 3 tablespoons chicken stock	1 teaspoon cornflour dissolved in 3 tablespoons chicken stock
oil for deep frying	oil for deep frying

Serves four
Preparation time: 20 minutes
Cooking time: 15 minutes

Cook the noodles in boiling, salted water for 10 minutes. Drain, then stir in 1 tablespoon of oil. Mix the soy sauce and sugar together in a bowl. Stir in the chicken and spring onions and set aside for 20 minutes. Heat the remaining oil in a large frying pan. Add the ginger and fry for 2 minutes. Add the vegetables and fry for 5 minutes. Stir in the cornflour mixture and the chicken mixture. Fry for a further 3-5 minutes, or until it is thoroughly heated. Place on serving dish and keep hot. Deep fry the noodles in the oil for 2-3 minutes or until crisp and golden brown. Drain on kitchen paper, then use to garnish the chicken mixture.

CREAMED CHICKEN CHINESE

Imperial	Metric
3-3½lb chicken	1.5kg chicken
1oz flour, seasoned	25g flour, seasoned
1oz butter	25g butter
1oz shelled and blanched almonds	25g shelled and blanched almonds
8oz can sliced bamboo shoots	225g can sliced bamboo shoots
salt	salt
pepper	pepper
¼ pint chicken stock	150ml chicken stock
4fl oz soured cream or fresh cream with 2 teaspoons lemon juice	125ml soured cream or fresh cream with 2 teaspoons lemon juice

Serves four to five
Preparation time: 15 minutes
Cooking time: 1 hour 30 minutes
Oven: 350°F, 180°C, Gas Mark 4

Dust the chicken with the seasoned flour. Melt the butter in a thick saucepan or iron casserole and brown the chicken quickly, turning it over and over, so that the whole bird is evenly browned. Chop the almonds into strips and brown them lightly in the remaining butter. Place the chicken, almonds, drained bamboo shoots and seasoning into a casserole, adding the stock. Cover and cook at 350°F (180°C, Gas Mark 4) for 1½ hours or until well cooked and tender. Half an hour before serving, remove the lid and pour the sour cream over the chicken, mixing it well with the gravy in the casserole. Baste the bird well with the mixture. Serve with boiled rice.

CHINESE WALNUT CHICKEN

Imperial	Metric
4oz chopped walnuts	100g chopped walnuts
3 tablespoons salad oil	3 tablespoons salad oil
8-12oz cooked chicken, cut into strips	225-350g cooked chicken, cut into strips
½ teaspoon salt	½ teaspoon salt
1 large onion, sliced	1 large onion, sliced
4 large celery stalks, sliced thinly	4 large celery stalks, sliced thinly
½ pint chicken stock	250ml chicken stock
1 tablespoon cornflour	1 tablespoon cornflour
1 teaspoon sugar	1 teaspoon sugar
3 tablespoons tamari soy sauce	3 tablespoons tamari soy sauce
2 tablespoons dry sherry	2 tablespoons dry sherry
1 small can water chestnuts, drained and sliced	1 small can water chestnuts, drained and sliced
2½oz can bamboo shoots, drained	65g can bamboo shoots, drained

Serves four
Preparation time: 15 minutes
Cooking time: 15 minutes

Fry walnuts in oil until golden, stirring continuously. Remove and drain. Add chicken to oil and fry for a few minutes. Remove and sprinkle with salt. To the same pan, add onion, celery, and half of the stock. Cook, uncovered, for about 5 minutes. Mix cornflour with sugar, soy sauce, sherry and remaining stock. Add to vegetables, cook, stirring continuously until sauce comes to the boil and thickens. Add water chestnuts, bamboo shoots and the walnuts. Replace chicken and heat through.

Above left: Crispy Noodles with Chicken and Vegetables
Above right: Chinese Walnut Chicken
Below centre: Creamed Chicken Chinese

INDIAN CHICKEN

Imperial	Metric
4 chicken portions	4 chicken portions
oil for frying	oil for frying
salt	salt
pepper	pepper

Sauce	**Sauce**
2 × 5fl oz cartons natural yoghurt	2 × 125ml cartons natural yoghurt
½ teaspoon ground ginger	½ teaspoon ground ginger
1 teaspoon curry powder	1 teaspoon curry powder
1 tablespoon cayenne pepper	1 tablespoon cayenne pepper
1 clove garlic	1 clove garlic
1-2 bay leaves	1-2 bay leaves
1 tablespoon tomato purée	1 tablespoon tomato purée
grated rind of 1 lemon	grated rind of 1 lemon
6-8oz saffron rice	150-225g saffron rice
dessicated coconut	dessicated coconut
sultanas	sultanas

Garnish	**Garnish**
sprigs of parsley	sprigs of parsley
slices of lemon	slices of lemon

Serves four
Preparation time: 10 minutes
Cooking time: 45 minutes

Season the chicken portions and fry in oil, or brush with oil and grill, until well browned all over and cooked through. Place in serving dish and keep warm. Mix together the yoghurt, ginger, curry powder, cayenne pepper, crushed garlic, bay leaves, tomato purée and lemon rind to a creamy sauce and heat very gently over a low heat until warmed through. Remove bay leaves and pour the sauce over chicken portions. Garnish with parsley and lemon slices. Serve with the rice cooked in boiling, salted water with a little saffron, and a dish of dessicated coconut mixed with sultanas.

SPANISH CHICKEN

Imperial	Metric
4½lb chicken	2kg chicken
oil	oil
salt	salt
pepper	pepper
1 teaspoon dried mixed herbs	1 teaspoon dried mixed herbs
8oz Spanish onions	225g Spanish onions
1lb green peppers, de-seeded and diced	450g green peppers, de-seeded and diced
4 tomatoes, peeled and roughly chopped	4 tomatoes, peeled and roughly chopped
2 cloves garlic, crushed	2 cloves garlic, crushed
8oz peas, cooked	225g peas, cooked
12oz long-grain rice	350g long-grain rice
pinch saffron powder	pinch saffron powder
1 bay leaf	1 bay leaf

Garnish	**Garnish**
2 whole prawns	2 whole prawns
lemon slices	lemon slices
chopped parsley	chopped parsley

Serves six
Preparation time: 20 minutes
Cooking time: 1 hour 50 minutes
Oven: 400°F, 200°C, Gas Mark 6

Rub the chicken with oil, sprinkle with salt, pepper and herbs and stand in a roasting pan. Pour a cup of water around the chicken. Cover loosely with aluminium foil and roast in a moderately hot oven, 400°F, (200°C, Gas Mark 6) for 1½ hours. Cool the chicken slightly, then strip the flesh from the bones, cut into bite-sized pieces and set aside. Use the carcass and giblets to make chicken stock in which to cook the rice. Fry the onions, peppers, tomatoes and garlic gently in the oil until soft and golden. Stir in the cooked drained peas. Cook the rice in 1½ pints (900ml) of chicken stock, with the saffron and bay leaf, for about 10 minutes, until tender. Drain if necessary (the rice should be quite dry) and remove the bay leaf. Now fold the chicken and rice into the onion mixture. Pile into a large, heated serving dish and garnish with the prawns and lemon slice. Serve sprinkled with parsley.

Left: Spanish Chicken
Centre: Indian Chicken
Right: Chicken with Sweetcorn

CHICKEN WITH SWEETCORN

Imperial	Metric
2 eggs, beaten	2 eggs, beaten
1lb can sweet corn	450g can sweet corn
4oz cheese, grated	100g cheese, grated
1 chicken, roasted or boiled	1 chicken, roasted or boiled
3oz carrots, cooked and diced	75g carrots, cooked and diced
8oz cooked French beans, fresh or frozen	225g cooked French beans, fresh or frozen
8oz cooked peas, fresh or frozen	225g cooked peas, fresh or frozen
1 level teaspoon salt	1 level teaspoon salt
¼ pint chicken stock	125ml chicken stock
2oz green olives, stoned and sliced	50g green olives, stoned and sliced
1oz seedless raisins	25g seedless raisins
½oz butter	15g butter
1 small or ½ green pepper, cut into strips	1 small or ½ green pepper, cut into strips
1 small or ½ red pepper, cut into strips	1 small or ½ red pepper, cut into strips

Serves four
Preparation time: 20 to 25 minutes
Cooking time: 30 to 40 minutes
Oven: 350°F, 180°C, Gas Mark 4

Combine eggs, corn and cheese in a bowl. Remove bones from chicken and cut meat into small pieces. In another bowl, combine chicken with vegetables, salt, stock, olives and raisins. Place a layer of corn mixture in a 3 pint (1.75 litre) greased casserole, then add a layer of the chicken mixture. Continue alternating layers, ending with a layer of corn. Dot top with butter, garnish with pepper strips, making a flower-like design. Bake in the oven 350°F (180°C, Gas Mark 3) for 30-40 minutes.

CHICKEN PORTUGAISE

Imperial	Metric
3 chicken quarters	3 chicken quarters
1-2 tablespoons oil	1-2 tablespoons oil
salt	salt
pepper	pepper
3 large tomatoes, peeled and sliced	3 large tomatoes, peeled and sliced
1½oz grated cheese	40g grated cheese
1 medium onion, peeled and sliced	1 medium onion, peeled and sliced

Serves three
Preparation time: 15 minutes
Cooking time: 50 minutes
Oven: 375°F, 190°C, Gas Mark 5

Brush the chicken quarters with oil, season well with salt and pepper and place in a casserole. Place the onion on top of the chicken, then the tomatoes and sprinkle with the grated cheese. Cook at 375°F (190°C, Gas Mark 5) for 50 minutes or until the chicken is tender. Remove the casserole lid for the last 10 minutes to brown the cheese. Serve hot with plain boiled vegetables or a green salad.

KABELI PILAU

Imperial	Metric
4lb cooked chicken	1.75kg cooked chicken
½lb long-grain rice	225g long-grain rice
salt	salt
2 large onions, sliced thinly	2 large onions, sliced thinly
1oz butter	25g butter
1 level teaspoon ground cardamom	1 level teaspoon ground cardamom
3 level teaspoons ground cumin	3 level teaspoons ground cumin
1 pint chicken stock	575ml chicken stock
3 carrots, cooked and sliced	3 carrots, cooked and sliced
4oz seedless raisins	100g seedless raisins

Serves six
Preparation time: 45 minutes
Cooking time: 30 minutes
Oven: 325°F, 160°C, Gas Mark 3

Remove chicken meat from bones, using only the large pieces for this dish. The remainder can be used in a soup or salad. Cook rice in boiling, salted water. Drain and rinse. To make sauce: Brown onions in hot butter and remove from heat. Add cardamom and cumin; mix to a paste with butter and onion. Add about 1 pint (575ml) stock, simmer for 5 minutes and taste for seasoning. Combine cooked rice, sauce and chicken pieces and place in a buttered casserole. Put carrots and raisins on top. Cover and cook in the oven, 325°F (160°C, Gas Mark 3), for about 30 minutes. Add more stock or water if dish becomes too dry. When done, mix carrots and raisins lightly with chicken and rice using a fork.

GRECIAN CHICKEN

Imperial	Metric
3¼lb chicken	1.5kg chicken
4oz streaky bacon, cut into pieces	100g streaky bacon, cut into pieces
1oz butter and olive oil mixed	25g butter and olive oil mixed
4oz stoned olives, preferably green, but black can be used	100g stoned olives, preferably green, but black can be used
4oz mushrooms, sliced	100g mushrooms, sliced
3 tablespoons sherry	3 tablespoons sherry
4 tomatoes, skinned and sliced	4 tomatoes, skinned and sliced
salt	salt
freshly ground pepper	freshly ground pepper

Serves four
Preparation time: 15 minutes
Cooking time: 1 hour 15 minutes
Oven: 350°F, 180°C, Gas Mark 4

Remove the giblets from the chicken and any fat from body cavity. Melt the butter and oil in a heavy pan and brown the chicken all over. Place the chicken in a warm casserole. Add the bacon and the mushrooms to the remaining fat in the pan, cook for 3-4 minutes, add the sherry and pour over the chicken. Season well with salt and black pepper and add the olives (if using black, soak in hot water for 15 minutes before using). Cover the casserole and cook in a moderate oven 350°F (180°C, Gas Mark 4) for 45 minutes. Add the slices of skinned tomato to the casserole, stir well, replace the lid and continue cooking for a further 30 minutes. If necessary, skim off any excess fat before serving.

N.B. This may also be cooked on top of the oven, in a pan with a tight fitting lid over a very gentle heat.

Above right: Grecian Chicken
Below left: Kabeli Pilau
Below right: Chicken Portugaise

CHICKEN CACCIATORE

Imperial	Metric
2 large or 4 small chicken thighs	2 large or 4 small chicken thighs
1oz butter	25g butter
2 tablespoons oil	2 tablespoons oil
1 large onion, diced	1 large onion, diced
1 clove garlic, crushed or finely chopped	1 clove garlic, crushed or finely chopped
4oz mushrooms, sliced	100g mushrooms, sliced
1 green pepper, diced	1 green pepper, diced
1 glass dry white wine	1 glass dry white wine
15oz can tomatoes	428g can tomatoes
salt	salt
pepper	pepper
1 teaspoon sugar	1 teaspoon sugar
1 teaspoon oregano or basil	1 teaspoon oregano or basil

Serves four
Preparation time: 20 minutes
Cooking time: 45 minutes

Sauté chicken thighs in oil and butter until brown on both sides. Add onion, garlic, mushrooms and green pepper. Cook for 3 minutes on low heat with lid on pan, stirring from time to time to prevent sticking. Add white wine and the can of tomatoes with liquor. Season with salt, pepper and sugar and add herbs. Continue simmering until chicken is tender. Serve with buttered tagliatelle.

ALMOND CHICKEN ARIMA

Imperial	Metric
1 onion, chopped	1 onion, chopped
¼ large cucumber, chopped	¼ large cucumber, chopped
3oz carrots, chopped	75g carrots, chopped
8oz canned water chestnuts, sliced	225g canned water chestnuts, sliced
8oz canned bamboo shoots	225g canned bamboo shoots
¼lb button mushrooms, halved	100g button mushrooms, halved
¾ pint boiling water	425ml boiling water
1lb raw or cooked chicken, cubed	450kg raw or cooked chicken, cubed
3 tablespoons olive oil	3 tablespoons olive oil
1 teaspoon salt	1 teaspoon salt
3oz almonds, blanched	75g almonds, blanched

Serves four to six
Preparation time: 20 minutes
Cooking time: 30 minutes

Left: Chicken Cacciatore
Centre: Almond Chicken Arima
Right: Chicken Crêpe Casserole

Combine onion, cucumber, carrots, water chestnuts, bamboo shoots and mushrooms. Add boiling water, cover and let stand for 10 minutes. Drain. Cook chicken in 2 tablespoons oil over low heat for 15-20 minutes or until tender. If using cooked chicken, then fry only for 2 or 3 minutes over low heat, stirring frequently. Add vegetables and salt. Blend and cook for 5 minutes. Cook almonds in remaining oil until golden brown. Pour chicken and vegetables into a hot serving dish and put the almonds on top. Serve immediately.

CHICKEN CREPE CASSEROLE

Imperial	Metric
12 pancakes, cooked one side only, made from:	12 pancakes, cooked one side only, made from:
6oz flour	150g flour
¾ pint milk	425ml milk
salt	salt
1 large egg	1 large egg

Filling	**Filling**
8oz spinach purée	225g spinach purée
4oz butter	100g butter
2oz mushrooms, finely chopped	50g mushrooms, finely chopped
1 onion, finely chopped	1 onion, finely chopped
8oz cooked chicken, cut into small pieces	225g cooked chicken, cut into small pieces
4 tablespoons Parmesan cheese	4 tablespoons Parmesan cheese
salt	salt
pepper	pepper
pinch tarragon or basil	pinch tarragon or basil
2oz flaked almonds	50g flaked almonds

Sauce	**Sauce**
½ pint chicken stock	250ml chicken stock
1oz flour	25g flour
1oz butter	25g butter
2 tablespoons white wine or sherry	2 tablespoons white wine or sherry

Serves six
Preparation time: 30 minutes
Cooking time: 20 to 30 minutes
Oven: 350°F, 180°C, Gas Mark 4

Make the sauce as for Macaroni Chicken, page 38, using stock and wine as liquid. Cook the spinach purée in a little butter. Sauté the mushrooms and onion in the rest of the butter. Mix chicken, spinach, mushrooms, onion, cheese and herbs and a quarter of the sauce together. Spoon a good tablespoon of filling on the unbrowned side of each pancake and roll up. Arrange pancakes with joins underneath, in greased shallow baking dish. Pour remaining sauce over pancakes and sprinkle with almonds. Bake in the oven at 350°F (180°C, Gas Mark 4) for 20-30 minutes.

POLYNESIAN TURKEY

Imperial	Metric
2 large or 4 small turkey joints	2 large or 4 small turkey joints
2 tablespoons oil	2 tablespoons oil
15oz can pineapple pieces	425g can pineapple pieces
1 tablespoon soya sauce	1 tablespoon soya sauce
2-3 sticks celery, chopped	2-3 sticks celery, chopped
1 onion, chopped	1 onion, chopped
1 level tbsp cornflour	1 level tbsp cornflour
3 tablespoons water	3 tablespoons water
2 tomatoes, skinned and cut into eighths	2 tomatoes, skinned and cut into eighths
1 green pepper, cut into rings	1 green pepper, cut into rings

Serves two
Cooking time: 1 hour

Heat oil in large frying pan and brown turkey joints on both sides for 15 minutes. Drain pineapple pieces and make up the juice to ¼ pint (150ml) with water. Remove turkey joints and keep warm. Fry the onion in the fat gently until clear. Add chopped celery and green pepper. Blend the cornflour with the water and add the pineapple juice and soya sauce. Add to the vegetables in the frying pan and bring to the boil. Add the pineapple pieces and tomato wedges and place the joints on top. Simmer for 30 minutes or until tender, stirring occasionally.
To serve: Place the turkey joints on a large warmed serving dish and spoon the sauce over.

ANDALUSIAN TURKEY

Imperial	Metric
3 anchovy fillets	3 anchovy fillets
4 tablespoons sherry	4 tablespoons sherry
black pepper, ground	black pepper, ground
8-10lb turkey	3.5-4.5kg turkey
10oz mushrooms	300g mushrooms
2oz green olives, stoned	50g green olives, stoned
the turkey liver	the turkey liver
salt and pepper	salt and pepper
8oz sausagemeat	225g sausagemeat
2oz butter, melted	50g butter, melted
slice of lemon	slice of lemon
2-3 tbsp fresh herbs	2-3 tbsp fresh herbs
2 slices streaky bacon	2 slices streaky bacon

To serve

Imperial	Metric
1oz butter for frying	25g butter for frying
6 slices bread, crusts removed, cut diagonally	6 slices bread, crusts removed, cut diagonally
1 small can foie gras	1 small can foie gras
1 small can whole chestnuts	1 small can whole chestnuts
green olives, halved and stoned, for garnish	green olives, halved and stoned, for garnish

Serves eight to ten
Preparation time: 30 minutes
Cooking time: 4 hours 30 minutes
Oven: 325°F, 160°C, Gas Mark 3

Crush the anchovies, mix them with 2 tablespoons sherry and grind of pepper and rub the bird inside with the mixture. Chop and mix the mushrooms, olives, liver, salt and pepper and sausagemeat; toss them in melted butter for a few minutes. Stuff the turkey and sew up the opening. Rub the turkey with the lemon slice and sprinkle it with the herbs. Cover the breast with bacon and aluminium foil. Cook the turkey in a moderate oven 325°F (160°C, Gas Mark 3) for 1 hour. Then remove the foil and baste with sherry. Continue basting regularly until the turkey is cooked — approximately 3-3½ hours. To serve: Melt the butter in a frying pan and fry the bread triangles. Spread half the slices with foie gras and the remainder with chestnuts. Arrange around the turkey. Garnish the turkey with halved green olives.

TANGERINE TURKEY

Imperial	Metric
10lb turkey	4.5kg turkey
1 onion, peeled and quartered	1 onion, peeled and quartered
2 carrots, skinned and sliced	2 carrots, skinned and sliced
2 sticks celery, cut into chunks	2 sticks celery, cut into chunks
2-3 tablespoons chopped parsley	2-3 tablespoons chopped parsley
1 bay leaf	1 bay leaf
salt and pepper	salt and pepper
4-5 tangerines	4-5 tangerines
4oz butter	100g butter
1 tablespoon flour	1 tablespoon flour
¼ pint single cream	150ml single cream

To Serve

Imperial	Metric
2lb rice, cooked	1kg rice, cooked
1oz butter	25g butter
4oz flaked almonds	100g flaked almonds
4oz raisins	100g raisins

Serves six to eight
Preparation time: 20 minutes
Cooking time: 1 hour 30 minutes to 2 hours

Joint the turkey into 8 portions (2 breasts, 2 thighs, 2 wings, 2 drumsticks) and put in a saucepan. Cover with water and bring to the boil gently. Skim off the froth and add carrots, onion, celery, parsley, bay leaf and salt and pepper. Cover and simmer until tender. While the turkey is cooking, grate the tangerine zest avoiding the bitter white pith until 3 tablespoons are obtained. Peel the tangerines, removing all the pith and divide into segments. Drain the turkey when tender, keeping back the stock for the sauce, and brown the joints in half of the butter. Place on a warmed serving dish, garnish with the tangerine segments and keep warm. Cook the rice. Heat the remaining butter, stir in the flour to make a roux and cook for a few minutes, without allowing it to brown, stirring continuously. Remove from the heat and gradually add ¼ pint (150ml) of the turkey stock. Stir in cream and tangerine zest and cook on a low heat for 3-4 minutes until the sauce thickens, stirring continuously. Pour over the turkey joints and serve with the rice. To serve the rice: Melt the butter in a frying pan and toss the almonds and raisins until hot. Stir into the rice.

Above left: Andalusian Turkey; Above right: Tangerine Turkey; Below centre: Polynesian Turkey

TURKEY WITH MUSHROOM & SAUSAGEMEAT STUFFING

Imperial	Metric
5-6lb turkey	2.5-3kg turkey
2oz butter, melted	50g butter, melted
salt	salt
black pepper	black pepper
Mushroom and Sausagemeat Stuffing	***Mushroom and Sausagemeat Stuffing***
1oz butter	25g butter
liver from the turkey, finely chopped	liver from the turkey, finely chopped
1 onion, finely chopped	1 onion, finely chopped
4oz button mushrooms, finely chopped	100g button mushrooms, finely chopped
1lb sausagemeat	450g sausagemeat
4oz fresh white breadcrumbs	100g fresh white breadcrumbs
4 level tablespoons cranberry sauce	4 level tablespoons cranberry sauce
1 level tablespoon fresh chopped parsley	1 level tablespoon fresh chopped parsley
salt	salt
pepper	pepper
1 egg, beaten	1 egg, beaten

Serves eight to ten
Preparation time: 30 minutes
Cooking time: 3 hours 30 minutes
Oven: 325°F, 160°C, Gas Mark 3

Wash the turkey and remove the giblets. Simmer the giblets except for the liver for 2 hours and use the liquid to make the gravy. Cover the bird with melted butter and seasoning. To make the stuffing: melt the butter and fry the liver, onions and mushrooms. Add liver and vegetables to sausagemeat with breadcrumbs, cranberry sauce, parsley, seasoning and beaten egg. Mix well. Stuff the turkey breast with the stuffing. Preheat the oven to 325°F (160°C, Gas Mark 3). Wrap the turkey loosely in aluminium foil and cook in the oven for 3 hours. Fold back the aluminium foil and cook for another 30 minutes to brown the breast. Serve with roast potatoes, bacon rolls, cranberry sauce, sprouts and well-flavoured giblet gravy.

CRANBERRY TURKEY CASSEROLE

Imperial	Metric
4 × 6oz pieces raw turkey	4 × 175g pieces raw turkey
a little seasoned flour	a little seasoned flour
3 tablespoons corn oil	3 tablespoons corn oil
8 small or 2 large onions	8 small or 2 large onions
2 sticks celery	2 sticks celery
2 tablespoons cornflour	2 tablespoons cornflour
1/2 pint turkey or chicken stock	275ml turkey or chicken stock
8oz can cranberry sauce	225g can cranberry sauce
4oz mushrooms, quartered	100g mushrooms, quartered

Above centre: Turkey Risotto
Below left: Turkey with Mushroom and Sausagemeat Stuffing
Below right: Cranberry Turkey Casserole

Serves four
Preparation time: 15 minutes if using whole bird
Cooking time: 2 hours
Oven: 350°F, 180°C, Gas Mark 3

Dust the turkey pieces in a little seasoned flour. Heat the oil in a frying pan and use to fry the turkey until lightly browned. Drain and remove to a casserole. Quarter the onions if large and cut the celery into 1-inch (2cm) lengths. Add these to the pan and fry for 2-3 minutes. Remove with a slotted spoon and put over the turkey. Stir the cornflour into the remaining oil in the pan and mix to a smooth paste. Gradually add the stock and cranberry sauce. Bring to the boil stirring constantly, and pour into the casserole. Cover and cook in a moderate oven 350°F, (180°C, Gas Mark 3) for 1½-2 hours, until tender. Add the mushrooms 15 minutes before the end of cooking time.

TURKEY RISOTTO

Imperial	Metric
8oz chopped turkey meat	225g chopped turkey meat
1oz butter	25g butter
1 onion, chopped	1 onion, chopped
1 level tablespoon curry powder	1 level tablespoon curry powder
½ level teaspoon mixed herbs	½ level teaspoon mixed herbs
salt	salt
pepper	pepper
pinch garlic salt	pinch garlic salt
1lb patna (long grain) rice	450g patna (long grain) rice
¾ pint stock (or water and stock cube)	425ml stock (or water and stock cube)

Garnish
1oz stuffed olives, sliced
¼lb peas, cooked

Garnish
25g stuffed olives, sliced
100g peas, cooked

Serves four
Preparation time: 30 minutes
Cooking time: 35 minutes

Melt butter in large pan and fry onion until transparent. Add the meat and cook for approximately 5 minutes or until browned lightly. Add curry powder, herbs, salt, pepper and garlic salt. Mix well and cook for 3 minutes. Add rice, mixing well. Pour stock in, bring to the boil, cover and cook for 35 minutes or until the rice has absorbed all the liquid. Add the olives and peas and serve.

BRAZILIAN DUCK WITH ORANGE

Imperial	Metric
4-5lb duck	2-2.5kg duck
salt	salt
pepper	pepper
juice of ½ lemon	juice of ½ lemon
1 small glass white wine	1 small glass white wine
3-4 oranges, peeled and sliced	3-4 oranges, peeled and sliced
2oz butter	50g butter

Serves four
Preparation time: 15 minutes (plus marinate overnight)
Cooking time: 2 hours
Oven: 375°F, 190°C, Gas Mark 5

Prepare the duck the day before it is needed by seasoning with salt and pepper, lemon juice and white wine and leave overnight. Rub the butter over the duck and cook at 375°F (190°C, Gas Mark 5), allowing 20 minutes per pound, until duck is tender. Baste frequently with the liquid. Cut into portions and put them on a hot serving dish. Skim fat from pan juices and pour the juices over the duck portions. Surround with sliced oranges and serve at once.

ROAST GOOSE

Imperial	Metric
6lb goose	2.75kg goose
salt	salt
pepper	pepper

Serves five
Preparation time: 10 minutes
Cooking time: 2 hours 30 minutes
Oven: 375°F, 190°C, Gas Mark 5

Prick skin of goose without piercing flesh and place bird in a roasting pan. Season with salt and pepper and roast at 375°F (190°C, Gas Mark 5), allowing 20-25 minutes per pound, or until the bird is tender. Serve with sage and onion forcemeat balls and apple sauce.

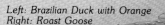

Left: Brazilian Duck with Orange
Right: Roast Goose

61

Special Occasions

CHICKEN WITH SHERRY AND ALMONDS

Imperial	Metric
3lb chicken, jointed	1.5kg chicken, jointed
¼ pint oil for frying	125ml oil for frying
1 large onion, chopped	1 large onion, chopped
approx. ¼ pint cooking sherry	approx. 125ml cooking sherry
about 1 pint chicken stock	about 500ml chicken stock
½ level teaspoon saffron	½ level teaspoon saffron
1 level tablespoon parsley, chopped	1 level tablespoon parsley, chopped
1 bay leaf	1 bay leaf
salt	salt
pepper	pepper
1 clove garlic, crushed	1 clove garlic, crushed
12 blanched almonds, finely chopped	12 blanched almonds, finely chopped
2 hardboiled egg yolks	2 hardboiled egg yolks
2 level tablespoons flour mixed with 4 tablespoons stock	2 level tablespoons flour mixed with 4 tablespoons stock
2 level tablespoons shredded ham	2 level tablespoons shredded ham

Serves four to six
Preparation time: 20 minutes
Cooking time: 45 minutes
Oven: 325°F, 160°C, Gas Mark 3

Fry the joints in oil until golden. Remove from pan and put into a saucepan. Fry the onion in the same fat and add to the chicken. Add sherry and then enough stock to just cover the chicken. Add saffron, chopped parsley and bay leaf. Cover tightly and cook over low heat until chicken is tender, or cook for 30-40 minutes in a very moderate oven 325°F (160°C, Gas Mark 3). Stir occasionally during cooking. Brown garlic in a little oil, make a paste of garlic, almonds and egg yolks by pounding in a mortar or grinding in a blender, add flour and stock mixture to paste and mix well. Remove chicken from pan, when tender, and slowly add paste to remaining stock, stirring constantly. Bring to boiling point, reduce heat and simmer for 5 minutes. Check and adjust seasoning if necessary. Add shredded ham and pour over chicken joints. Serve immediately accompanied by fluffy rice or potatoes and a green vegetable.

GINGERED CHICKEN

Imperial	Metric
2 teaspoons flour	2 teaspoons flour
1/4 teaspoon powdered ginger	1/4 teaspoon powdered ginger
cook-bag	cook-bag
2 1/2 lb chicken	1.1kg chicken
6oz rice	175g rice
saffron	saffron
Glaze	**Glaze**
4 tablespoons sliced stem ginger in syrup	4 tablespoons sliced stem ginger in syrup
1 tablespoon lemon juice	1 tablespoon lemon juice
3 tablespoons sherry	3 tablespoons sherry
1/2 oz butter	15g butter
Garnish	**Garnish**
almonds	almonds
maraschino cherries	maraschino cherries

Serves four
Preparation time: 20 minutes
Cooking time: 1 hour 15 minutes
Oven: 400°F, 200°C, Gas Mark 6

Mix together the flour and powdered ginger and use to dust the inside of the cook-bag. Place the chicken in the bag and follow the packet instructions. Cook in the oven at 400°F (200°C, Gas Mark 6) for 1 1/2 hours. Cook the rice in boiling salted water with a little saffron until tender. Put the stem ginger, syrup, lemon juice, sherry and butter in a small saucepan, bring to the boil and simmer until reduced to a syrup. After cooking the chicken, remove from the bag and divide the chicken in half lengthways. Place the chicken on the rice, pour the glaze over and decorate with the sliced stem ginger, almonds and maraschino cherries.

ROAST CHICKEN WITH APRICOT AND ALMOND STUFFING

Imperial	Metric
1oz butter	25g butter
1oz almonds, chopped finely	25g almonds, chopped finely
1 stick celery, finely chopped	1 stick celery, finely chopped
2oz apple, chopped	50g apple, chopped
1 small onion, finely chopped	1 small onion, finely chopped
2oz white breadcrumbs	50g white breadcrumbs
3oz apricots, either dried apricots, soaked overnight or tinned apricots	75g apricots, either dried apricots, soaked overnight or tinned apricots
salt	salt
pepper	pepper
1 egg, beaten	1 egg beaten
3lb chicken	1.5kg chicken
Garnish	**Garnish**
1 1/2 oz slivered almonds	40g slivered almonds
large can apricot halves	large can apricot halves
small bunch watercress	small bunch watercress

Serves six
Preparation time: 15 minutes
Cooking time: 1 hour 50 minutes
Oven: 375°F, 190°C, Gas Mark 5

Melt the butter and add the nuts, fry gently until they begin to colour. Add the celery, apple and onion and fry gently for 2 or 3 minutes. Mix in the breadcrumbs, chop the apricots and add seasoning. Bind the mixture together with the beaten egg, using sufficient to hold the mixture together. Stuff the neck cavity of the bird and then roast in the oven 375°F (190°C, Gas Mark 5), for about 1 hour 20 minutes, basting from time to time. When the chicken is nearing the completion of its cooking time, brown a few slivered almonds on a baking tray in the oven with the chicken and place the apricot halves in the oven to heat through. Serve the chicken on a dish and garnish by placing the drained apricot halves all round it and sprinkle them with the browned almonds. Add a small bunch of watercress for extra colour.

Left: Gingered Chicken
Above centre: Chicken with Sherry and Almonds
Right: Roast Chicken with Apricot and Almond Stuffing

Summer Barbecue for Eight People

DEVILLED CHICKEN

Imperial	Metric
1 level tablespoon tomato sauce	1 level tablespoon tomato sauce
1 level tablespoon French mustard	1 level tablespoon French mustard
4 level tablespoons chutney, chopped	4 level tablespoons chutney, chopped
2 level tablespoons fresh white breadcrumbs	2 level tablespoons fresh white breadcrumbs
salt	salt
pepper	pepper
8 chicken joints	8 chicken joints
2oz butter, melted	50g butter, melted

Preparation time: 1 hour 20 minutes
Cooking time: 30 minutes

Mix together tomato ketchup, mustard, chutney, breadcrumbs and seasoning. Make 3 or 4 deep slits in the flesh of each chicken joint. Fill each slit with a little of the devilled mixture. Cover joints and leave in a cool place for at least an hour, or preferably overnight, for chicken to absorb flavours. Brush chicken with melted butter and wrap each one in aluminium foil to make a parcel. Barbecue until well cooked. Open up foil to brown the chicken skin for the last 3 minutes.

CHICKEN DRUMSTICKS WITH BARBECUE SAUCE

Imperial	Metric
½ pint cider	300ml cider
2 level teaspoons French mustard	2 level teaspoons French mustard
1 small onion or shallot, chopped	1 small onion or shallot, chopped
1 clove garlic, finely chopped	1 clove garlic, finely chopped
½ small green pepper	½ small green pepper
salt	salt
pepper	pepper
8 chicken drumsticks	8 chicken drumsticks
1 level tablespoon cornflour	1 level tablespoon cornflour

Preparation time: 4 hours 15 minutes
Cooking time: 30 minutes

Mix together the cider, mustard, onion, garlic, green pepper and seasoning. Place chicken drumsticks in a large ovenproof casserole dish, and pour cider mixture over chicken. Cover and leave in a cool place for at least 4 hours to marinate. Drain off drumsticks and wrap aluminium foil around the joints. Keep cool until required. Meanwhile, pour cider mixture into a small saucepan, mix cornflour with a little cold water, add to saucepan, and stir. Bring to the boil and cook for a minute, stirring. Cover and keep until required. At the barbecue, cook the chicken drumsticks until well done and heat up the sauce.

HERB AND GARLIC BREAD

Imperial	Metric
1 Vienna or French loaf	1 Vienna or French loaf
4oz butter	100g butter
1 clove garlic, crushed	1 clove garlic, crushed
¼ teaspoon oregano	¼ teaspoon oregano
1 level tablespoon fresh chopped parsley	1 level tablespoon fresh chopped parsley
1 level tablespoon grated Parmesan cheese	1 level tablespoon grated Parmesan cheese

Preparation time: 15 minutes
Cooking time: 5 minutes

Cut the bread diagonally in ½-inch (2cm) slices, almost but not quite through the bottom crust. Mix together the butter, garlic, oregano, parsley and cheese. Spread on both sides of each bread slice. Wrap the loaf completely in aluminium foil. Heat over barbecue.

BARBECUE DIP

Imperial	Metric
¼ pint mayonnaise	125ml mayonnaise
1 small onion, minced	1 small onion, minced
4 gherkins, minced	4 gherkins, minced
1 teaspoon Yorkshire Relish	1 teaspoon Yorkshire Relish
1 teaspoon vinegar	1 teaspoon vinegar
3 teaspoons soya sauce	3 teaspoons soya sauce

Preparation time: 3 hours 15 minutes

Put all ingredients into a bowl and blend well together. Chill for 3 hours.

PIQUANT SAUCE

Imperial	Metric
1oz butter	25g butter
1 medium onion, chopped	1 medium onion, chopped
1oz flour	25g flour
4 tablespoons cider	4 tablespoons cider
2 tablespoons vinegar	2 tablespoons vinegar
½ pint stock	300ml stock
2 tablespoons tomato sauce	2 tablespoons tomato sauce
2 tablespoons soya sauce	2 tablespoons soya sauce
2 tablespoons sugar	2 tablespoons sugar
salt and pepper	salt and pepper

Preparation and Cooking time: 20 minutes

Cook onion in the butter. Stir in the flour. Add the cider, vinegar and stock. Bring to the boil. Add the tomato and soya sauce and sugar. Simmer until thick, then season to taste. When required, heat and serve hot.
VEGETABLES: Cut green peppers, tomatoes and onions into either halves or quarters. Arrange decoratively on skewers, brush with oil and barbecue.

*Above centre: Devilled Chicken; Above left: Piquant Sauce; Above right: Barbecue Dip
Below centre: Chicken drumsticks with barbecue sauce; Below left: Herb and Garlic Bread*

ROAST TURKEY WITH CRANBERRY STUFFING

Imperial	Metric
10lb turkey	4.5kg turkey
little cooking oil or melted butter	little cooking oil or melted butter
Stuffing	**Stuffing**
¼lb fresh white breadcrumbs	100g fresh white breadcrumbs
6oz prunes, pre-soaked and chopped	175g prunes, pre-soaked and chopped
1 large apple, peeled and diced	1 large apple, peeled and diced
1½oz almonds, blanched and chopped	40g almonds, blanched and chopped
2 tablespoons whole berry cranberry sauce	2 tablespoons whole berry cranberry sauce
grated rind and juice of ½ lemon	grated rind and juice of ½ lemon
1 egg, beaten	1 egg, beaten
1 tablespoon cooking oil	1 tablespoon cooking oil
Garnish	**Garnish**
6 medium-sized Cox's apples, cored and left whole	6 medium-sized Cox's apples, cored and left whole
6 tablespoons whole berry cranberry sauce	6 tablespoons whole berry cranberry sauce
watercress	watercress
Cranberry sauce	**Cranberry sauce**
8-12oz cranberries — thaw frozen cranberries thoroughly	225-350 cranberries — thaw frozen cranberries thoroughly
¼ pint water	150ml water
2-3oz sugar	50-75g sugar
a little port (optional)	a little port (optional)

Serves eight to ten
Preparation time: 35 minutes
Cooking time: 4 hours 30 minutes
Oven: 325°F, 160°C, Gas Mark 3

For stuffing, put breadcrumbs in a bowl, add prunes, apple, almonds, cranberry sauce and juice and rind of lemon. Bind together all the ingredients with the beaten egg and oil. Stuff the neck cavity of the bird and hold the skin in place with a small skewer. Place the turkey in a greased roasting pan. Brush with melted butter or oil and sprinkle with salt. Cover with a square of aluminium foil. Place in a pre-heated oven at 325°F (160°C, Gas Mark 3) and roast for 3 hours 45 minutes. Remove the foil, baste and return to the oven for 45 minutes to brown all over. Half an hour before the end of the cooking time, score the apples by removing thin strips of skin with either a cannelling knife or by marking two score lines with a sharp knife approximately ½-inch (1cm) apart all round the apple and removing the strips of skin between them. Place 1 tablespoon of cranberry sauce in the centre of each apple and bake for 20-25 minutes in the oven with the turkey, until tender but not too soft. Remove the turkey, drain and serve, garnished with the scored apples and watercress.

Cranberry sauce: make a syrup by dissolving the sugar in the water and boiling for 5 minutes. Add the cranberries and simmer for about 10 minutes or until it thickens. Stir in port, if used. Cool before serving.

69

EASTER TURKEY

Imperial	Metric
6lb turkey	3kg turkey
1½oz butter	40g butter
2 onions, sliced	2 onions, sliced
2 carrots, sliced	2 carrots, sliced
3 sticks of celery, chopped (reserve leaves for garnish)	3 sticks of celery, chopped (reserve leaves for garnish)
3 rashers of bacon, roughly chopped	3 rashers of bacon, roughly chopped
½ bottle red wine	½ bottle red wine
½-¾ pint chicken or turkey stock	275-425ml chicken or turkey stock
bouquet garni	bouquet garni
salt	salt
pepper	pepper

Serves eight
Preparation time: 20 minutes
Cooking time: 3-3 hours 30 minutes
Oven: 325°F, 160°C, Gas Mark 3

Melt the butter in a large flameproof casserole and cook the onions, carrots, celery, and bacon for a few minutes. Add the bouquet garni and seasoning. Place the turkey on top and pour over the red wine and enough stock to come half way up the bird. Cover the casserole with a lid and cook in the oven 325°F (160°C, Gas Mark 3) for 3-3½ hours turning from side to side every ½ hour to allow all sides to cook equally. Remove the bouquet garni from the casserole. Boil up the juices and vegetables until they reduce slightly. Place the turkey on a serving dish, surround with vegetables and juice. Garnish with the celery leaves.

ROAST STUFFED GOOSE

Imperial	Metric
7lb goose	3kg goose
flour for sprinkling	flour for sprinkling
giblets and neck, simmered for stock	giblets and neck, simmered for stock

Stuffing

Imperial	Metric
8oz long-grain rice, three-quarters cooked in boiling salted water, drained and dried	225g long-grain rice, three-quarters cooked in boiling salted water, drained and dried
2 onions peeled and chopped	2 onions peeled and chopped
8oz prunes, stewed, stoned and chopped	225g prunes, stewed, stoned and chopped
the goose liver, blanched in boiling water and chopped	the goose liver, blanched in boiling water and chopped
salt	salt
pepper	pepper
grated rind of 1 lemon	grated rind of 1 lemon
1 egg	1 egg

Serves eight
Preparation time: 20 minutes
Cooking time: 3 hours 10 minutes
Oven: 425°F, 220°C, Gas Mark 7, then
350°F, 180°C, Gas Mark 4

Make the stuffing by mixing together the rice, onion, prunes, chopped liver, seasoning and lemon rind. Bind together with the egg. Stuff the goose and sprinkle lightly with the flour. Prick the skin all over but do not pierce the flesh. Put the goose in a roasting pan and cook in a fairly hot oven 425°F (220°C, Gas Mark 7) for 15 minutes. Reduce the heat to 350°F (180°C, Gas Mark 4) and continue roasting, allowing about 25 minutes per pound until goose is tender.

When cooked, put goose on a dish and keep hot. Pour off the fat and add the giblet stock to the juices that are left in the roasting pan. Bring to boil and then strain into a gravy boat and serve with the goose.

DUCK WITH ORANGE SAUCE

Imperial	Metric
4-5lb duck	1.75-2.5kg duck
salt	salt
pepper	pepper
1 small onion, peeled and sliced	1 small onion, peeled and sliced
1 small apple, peeled and sliced	1 small apple, peeled and sliced
1 clove garlic, peeled	1 clove garlic, peeled
¼ pint chicken stock	150ml chicken stock
2-3 tablespoons brandy	2-3 tablespoons brandy
juice of 1 lemon	juice of 1 lemon
3 oranges	3 oranges
2 tablespoons sugar	2 tablespoons sugar
2 tablespoons water	2 tablespoons water
rind of 1 orange, cut into thin strips, blanched in boiling water	rind of 1 orange, cut into thin strips, blanched in boiling water
Garnish	**Garnish**
watercress	watercress

Serves four
Preparation time: 20 minutes
Cooking time: 2 hours 30 minutes
Oven: 375°F, 190°C, Gas Mark 5

Wipe the duck with a clean, damp cloth and sprinkle the inside with salt and pepper. Put the onion and apple in the cavity and prick the skin of the bird with a fork without piercing the flesh. Rub the clove of garlic over it and sprinkle with salt and pepper. Put the duck in a roasting pan and cook at 375°F (190°C, Gas Mark 5), allowing 20-25 minutes per pound. Remove the duck and keep hot. Skim the fat from the juices in the pan and add chicken stock, scraping all the sediment from base of pan. Add the brandy the juice of the lemon and of the oranges. Put the water and sugar in another pan and boil until sugar just turning to caramel and is a rich golden brown. Add this to the sauce and continue to simmer gently until the sauce is reduced by half. Carve the duck and place on a hot serving dish. Strain the sauce over it and sprinkle with the orange rind. Garnish with watercress and serve at once.

Left: Duck with Orange Sauce
Above right: Easter Turkey
Below right: Roast Stuffed Goose

Meals in a Hurry

CHICKEN PARCELS

Imperial	Metric
4 chicken quarters	4 chicken quarters
little wine, cream or stock	little wine, cream or stock
2oz chopped bacon	50g chopped bacon
2oz chopped mushrooms	50g chopped mushrooms
1oz chopped onion	25g chopped onion
(all mixed together)	(all mixed together)
salt	salt
pepper	pepper

Serves four
Preparation time: 10 to 15 minutes
Cooking time: 45 minutes
Oven: 375°F, 190°C, Gas Mark 5

Mix the bacon, mushrooms and onion together and, for each portion, place a tablespoon on to a square of buttered or oiled aluminium foil. Season lightly. Place a chicken portion on top and pour over 1 tablespoon of wine, cream or stock. Close the foil loosely and cook on a baking tray at 375°F (190°C, Gas Mark 5) for about 45 minutes, opening the foil for the last 10 minutes to allow the portions to brown.

CHICKEN RISSOLES

Imperial	Metric
1 chicken stock cube	1 chicken stock cube
16fl oz boiling water	450ml boiling water
1 large packet instant mashed potato (4-6 servings)	1 large packet instant mashed potato (4-6 servings)
12oz cooked chicken, finely chopped	350g cooked chicken, finely chopped
8oz can cranberry sauce, mango chutney or apple sauce	225g can cranberry sauce, mango chutney or apple sauce
salt	salt
pepper	pepper
beaten egg	beaten egg
breadcrumbs	breadcrumbs
oil for frying	oil for frying

Serves four
Preparation time: 25 to 30 minutes
Cooking time: 10 to 15 minutes

Dissolve the stock cube in the boiling water. Use this to make up the mashed potato as directed on the packet. Add the chicken and sauce or chutney to the potato and season to taste. Form the mixture into 12 rissoles and coat with egg and breadcrumbs. Heat the oil in a frying pan and fry the rissoles on both sides until golden brown. Serve hot with vegetables or salad.

QUICK CHICKEN PIE

Imperial	Metric
8-10oz leftover cooked chicken meat	225-275g leftover cooked chicken meat
1oz butter or margarine	25g butter or margarine
1oz flour	25g flour
½ pint milk	275ml milk
salt	salt
pepper	pepper
1 tablespoon cooked peas	1 tablespoon cooked peas
1 tablespoon cooked, diced carrot	1 tablespoon cooked, diced carrot
1 tablespoon of any other suitable cooked vegetable	1 tablespoon of any other suitable cooked vegetable
6oz shortcrust pastry (made with 4oz flour, 1oz butter or margarine and 1oz lard)	150g shortcrust pastry (made with 100g flour, 25g butter or margarine and 25g lard)
little beaten egg or milk	little beaten egg or milk

Serves three to four
Preparation time: 20 minutes
Cooking time: 20 to 25 minutes
Oven: 425°F, 220°C, Gas Mark 7
        Reduce to 375°F, 190°C, Gas Mark 5

Melt the butter or margarine and add the flour, cook gently for 2-3 minutes but do not allow to brown. Remove the pan from the heat and add the milk gradually, stirring all the time. Bring to the boil and cook for a further 1-2 minutes, stirring continuously. Season well. Add the diced, cooked chicken, and the cooked vegetables. Pour into a deep pie dish and cover with the pastry. Brush the top with a little beaten egg or milk. Place in a hot oven 425°F (220°C, Gas Mark 7) for 10 minutes and then reduce the heat to moderate 375°F (190°C, Gas Mark 5) and cook for a further 20-25 minutes or until the pastry is crisp and golden.

Above left: Chicken Rissoles
Below left: Chicken Parcels
Right: Quick Chicken Pie

CHICKEN LIVER KEBABS

Imperial	Metric
4oz chicken livers	100g chicken livers
5 rashers streaky bacon	5 rashers streaky bacon
6 button mushrooms	6 button mushrooms
piece of tinned pimento or fresh red pepper	piece of tinned pimento or fresh red pepper
salt	salt
pepper	pepper
1 tablespoon oil	1 tablespoon oil
6 squares of onion or 6 small pickling onions	6 squares of onion or 6 small pickling onions

Serves four
Preparation time: 25 minutes
Cooking time: 10 minutes

Cut livers into pieces; cut the bacon rashers in half, and roll them up. Cut the pimento or red pepper into bite-sized pieces. Allow one skewer per person and thread on the pieces of bacon, liver, onion, mushrooms and pimento. Season lightly, brush with oil and grill for about 10 minutes, turning frequently. Serve with boiled rice.

STUFFED PEPPERS

Imperial	Metric
4 medium green peppers	4 medium green peppers
1 tablespoon oil	1 tablespoon oil
¼lb mushrooms	100g mushrooms
1 small onion	1 small onion
8oz cooked chicken, finely diced	225g cooked chicken, finely diced
½ teaspoon mixed herbs	½ teaspoon mixed herbs
salt	salt
pepper	pepper
1 beaten egg	1 beaten egg

Serves four
Preparation time: 30 minutes
Cooking time: 20 minutes
Oven: 350°F, 180°C, Gas Mark 4

Cut the tops off the peppers at the stalk end. Remove all the seeds and the core and place them in boiling water for about 5 minutes, then rinse them in cold water and leave them upside down to drain. Heat the oil and cook the mushrooms gently until soft and then chop them finely. Grate the onion and mix it well with the chicken, mushrooms and herbs. Season the mixture well and then bind it all together with the beaten egg. Pack the filling into the peppers. Take an ovenproof dish and pour in enough hot water to cover the bottom. Place the peppers in the dish and cover them with a piece of foil. Bake at 350°F (180°C, Gas Mark 4) for about 20 minutes or until the peppers are tender.

Left: Chicken Liver Kebabs
Centre: Stuffed Peppers
Right: Chicken and Mushroom Flan

CHICKEN AND MUSHROOM FLAN

Imperial	Metric
Flan Case	**Flan Case**
4oz packet instant potato	125g packet instant potato
½ beaten egg	½ beaten egg
Filling	**Filling**
6oz mushrooms	150g mushrooms
2oz butter or margarine	50g butter or margarine
3oz lean bacon	75g lean bacon
1oz plain flour	25g plain flour
½ pint milk	250ml milk
6-8oz cooked chicken, chopped	150-225g cooked chicken, chopped
salt	salt
pepper	pepper
2 tomatoes	2 tomatoes
sprig of parsley	sprig of parsley

Serves four to six
Preparation time: 15 minutes
Cooking time: 50 minutes
Oven: 400°F, 200°C, Gas Mark 6

Flan Case: Make up the instant potato as directed on the packet, beat in the egg. Line a well-greased 8-inch (20cm) flan ring or shallow ovenware dish with the mixture. Bake in the oven 400°F (200°C, Gas Mark 6) for 15 minutes.

Filling: Carefully wipe the mushrooms and leave whole; melt half the butter and brush over the mushrooms. Grill the mushrooms and bacon. Make a white sauce with the flour, remaining butter and the milk. Remember to add the milk slowly at first after melting the butter and adding the flour — it is a good idea to leave a little milk in case the sauce is too thin: it can be added after the sauce has thickened if it is needed.

Reserve 4 mushrooms for garnishing and chop the remainder with the bacon. Add the chicken, chopped mushrooms and bacon to the sauce and season well with salt and pepper. Spread the mixture in the cooked flan case. Garnish with the whole mushrooms, thin slices of tomato and a sprig of parsley. Serve hot.

CHICKEN OPEN SANDWICHES

Place a lettuce leaf on buttered bread. Cut the meat into small pieces and mix with sufficient mayonnaise to bind together. Pile on top of the lettuce. Garnish with slices of stuffed olives and watercress.

OR: Mix a little cranberry sauce with some thick mayonnaise and use to spread on the bread in place of butter. Top with lettuce and slices of meat and garnish with a twisted slice of cucumber.

OR: Arrange some shredded lettuce on buttered bread and top with slices of red pepper or tomato and sliced meat. Finish with mango chutney.

Serves as many as required
Preparation time: 20 to 30 minutes

CHICKEN PIZZA

Imperial	Metric
12oz bread or scone dough	350g bread or scone dough
2 tablespoons oil	2 tablespoons oil
1 onion, finely chopped	1 onion, finely chopped
1 clove garlic, crushed	1 clove garlic, crushed
1 large can peeled tomatoes	1 large can peeled tomatoes
1 teaspoon mixed dried herbs	1 teaspoon mixed dried herbs
6oz cooked chicken, finely diced	150g cooked chicken, finely diced
salt	salt
pepper	pepper
1 level tablespoon cornflour	1 level tablespoon cornflour
2-3oz cheese, grated or in slices	50-75g cheese, grated or in slices

Serves four to six
Preparation time: 30 minutes
Cooking time: 20-25 minutes
Oven: 400°F, 200°C, Gas Mark 6

Make up the bread or scone dough. Heat the oil in a saucepan, add the onion and garlic and fry for 3-4 minutes. Add the tomatoes, herbs and seasoning and simmer gently for 15 minutes. Stir in the diced meat. Blend the cornflour with 2 tablespoons water and stir into the tomato mixture, then stir over the heat until thickened. Roll out the dough to a large circle not more than ¼-inch (0.5cm) thick. Place on a baking tray. Spread the tomato mixture over the top, and place the cheese over the tomato. Bake in a hot oven 400°F (200°C, Gas Mark 6) for 20-25 minutes until golden brown. Garnish with strips of anchovy fillet and black or green olives.

CHICKEN AND HAM PATTIES

Imperial	Metric
4oz lean bacon or cooked ham	100g lean bacon or cooked ham
7oz cooked chicken	200g cooked chicken
pinch of mixed herbs	pinch of mixed herbs
1oz butter	25g butter
2 tablespoons flour	2 tablespoons flour
6 tablespoons chicken stock	6 tablespoons chicken stock
salt	salt
pepper	pepper
3 tablespoons milk	3 tablespoons milk
1 egg, beaten	1 egg, beaten
8oz frozen puff pastry	225g frozen puff pastry
Glaze	**Glaze**
milk or beaten egg	milk or beaten egg

Serves four
Preparation time: 35 minutes
Cooking time: 10-15 minutes
Oven: 450°F, 230°C, Gas Mark 8

If bacon is used, grill until cooked. Drain off fat. Cool. Chop chicken and ham (or bacon) and add herbs. Melt the butter in pan and make a roux with the flour, stirring well and cooking gently for 3 or 4 minutes, taking care not to let it brown. Stir in the chicken stock, with seasoning, boil for 4 or 5 minutes and add the milk. Remove from the heat, cool slightly, then add the egg, ready beaten. Return to a very gentle heat and cook slowly for 3 minutes. Mix in the chopped meat and leave to get cold. Meanwhile, roll out the pastry. Cut into eight 4-inch (10cm) rounds. Line 4 patty tins with pastry rounds. Spoon some of the cold mixture into each, cover with remaining pastry rounds, moistening the edges and pressing firmly together. Prick several times on top with a fork, brush with milk or beaten egg, and bake in the oven at 450°F (230°C, Gas Mark 8) for 10 to 15 minutes until golden brown. Serve either hot or cold.

Above centre: Chicken Open Sandwiches
Below left: Chicken and Ham Patties
Below right: Chicken Pizza

MID-WEEK CHICKEN

Imperial	Metric
3lb chicken or 4 chicken quarters	1.5kg chicken or 4 chicken quarters
salt	salt
pepper	pepper
2 tablespoons oil	2 tablespoons oil
1 large can tomatoes	1 large can tomatoes
1 medium onion, peeled and sliced	1 medium onion, peeled and sliced
1 green pepper, de-seeded and cut into strips	1 green pepper, de-seeded and cut into strips
4oz button mushrooms	100g button mushrooms
1/2 teaspoon oregano (optional)	1/2 teaspoon oregano (optional)

Serves four
Preparation time: 25 minutes
Cooking time: 30 minutes

Cut the chicken into 4 quarters and season well. Heat the oil in a frying pan and fry the chicken until brown on all sides. Add the remaining ingredients, cover and simmer, stirring occasionally for about 30 minutes, until chicken is cooked and sauce has thickened.

CHICKEN SUPREME

Imperial	Metric
2 cooked chicken breasts	2 cooked chicken breasts
1/2oz butter	15g butter
1 level tablespoon flour	1 level tablespoon flour
1/4 pint chicken stock	150ml chicken stock
salt	salt
pepper	pepper
1 egg yolk	1 egg yolk
5 tablespoons single cream	5 tablespoons single cream
squeeze of lemon juice	squeeze of lemon juice

Serves two
Preparation time: 20 minutes
Cooking time: 10 to 15 minutes
Oven: 325°F, 160°C, Gas Mark 3

Melt the butter and add the flour, cook gently until pale straw colour, but do not allow to brown. Blend in the stock, stirring all the time, bring to the boil and then simmer for 1 minute. Season. Blend the cream and the egg yolk and stir in a little of the hot sauce. Mix the egg yolk and cream mixture into the remainder of the sauce with a squeeze of lemon juice. Place the chicken breasts in a small shallow ovenproof dish and pour the sauce over them. Heat in a low oven approximately 325°F (160°C, Gas Mark 3) until the breasts are heated through but being careful not to boil the sauce as it will curdle. Alternatively, the breasts can be heated through in the sauce on the top of the oven, again being careful not to boil. Serve immediately with carrots or a green vegetable and potatoes.

EMPANADAS — INDIVIDUAL CHICKEN PIES

Imperial	Metric
8oz plain flour	225g plain flour
1 large or 2 small eggs, lightly beaten	1 large or 2 small eggs, lightly beaten
4oz suet, finely chopped	100g suet, finely chopped
water to mix with 1 level teaspoon salt	water to mix with 1 level teaspoon salt
1 large onion, chopped	1 large onion, chopped
1lb chicken, raw or cooked and chopped	450g chicken, raw or cooked and chopped
2oz sweet red peppers, fresh or tinned, chopped	50g sweet red peppers, fresh or tinned, chopped
16 small stuffed olives	16 small stuffed olives
2oz raisins	50g raisins
1 hardboiled egg, chopped	1 hardboiled egg, chopped
salt	salt
pepper	pepper

Serves eight
Preparation time: 45 minutes
Cooking time: 25 minutes
Oven: 350°F, 180°C, Gas Mark 8

Combine the flour, egg and half the suet. Mix in the salted water until the dough has a consistency capable of being rolled into very thin sheets. Put the onion, chicken, red peppers and remaining suet in a pan and fry until the onions and chicken are tender. If cooked chicken is used, add to pan after onions have been cooked. Add olives, raisins and chopped egg. Season to taste. Roll out the dough into very thin sheets and cut into 8 × 5 inch (20cm × 12.5cm) squares for individual empanadas. Place a tablespoon of chicken mixture on each square. Fold dough over meat and press edges together. Place on greased baking sheet and bake for about 25 minutes in a moderate oven 350°F (180°C, Gas Mark 4) until crisp and golden brown. Serve with winter salad or a salad of your own choice.

Above left: Chicken Supreme
Above right: Empanadas
Below centre: Mid-week Chicken

SUSSEX CHICKEN JOINTS

Imperial	Metric
2½lb chicken, cut into quarters or 4 chicken quarters	1.1kg chicken, cut into quarters or 4 chicken quarters
salt	salt
3oz butter	75g butter
1 clove garlic, crushed or ¼ teaspoon mixed herbs	1 clove garlic, crushed or ¼ teaspoon mixed herbs
2 small packets potato crisps, plain	2 small packets potato crisps, plain
1oz grated cheese	25g grated cheese

Serves four
Preparation time: 20 minutes
Cooking time: 40 minutes
Oven: 350°F, 180°C, Gas Mark 4

Sprinkle the quarters with salt. Melt the butter in a saucepan with the garlic or herbs. Crush the crisps and mix with the grated cheese. Dip the quarters in the melted butter and coat evenly with the crisp crumbs and cheese. Arrange the chicken in the base of a shallow baking tin, so they do not overlap, and trickle any of the remaining butter mixture over them. Bake uncovered for about 40 minutes and serve them hot or cold with crisp green salad or coleslaw.

GRILLED CHICKEN WITH SOUR CREAM SAUCE

Imperial	Metric
2½lb chicken	1.1kg chicken
2oz melted butter	50g melted butter
Sauce	**Sauce**
½ pint soured cream or fresh cream plus 1 tablespoon lemon juice	275ml soured cream or fresh cream plus 1 tablespoon lemon juice
2 egg yolks	2 egg yolks
salt	salt
ground black pepper	ground black pepper
paprika	paprika

Serves three to four
Preparation time: 10 to 15 minutes
Cooking time: 40 minutes

Cut the chicken right through the backbone and flatten it out, skewering it flat if necessary. Season the bird well on both sides and then place it, cut side up, in the bottom of the grill pan. Brush it over with melted butter. Turn the grill to high and grill the bird for 5 minutes, then turn over, brush again with butter and grill for a further 5 minutes. Reduce the heat and continue cooking and turning until the bird is well cooked and tender, about another 25 or 30 minutes. Meanwhile, heat the cream gently with the egg yolks until thickened but on no account allow to boil. Season and then put into a sauce boat and sprinkle the top with paprika. Serve with the chicken.

LEFTOVER TURKEY IN CHESTNUT SAUCE

Imperial	Metric
8 slices cooked turkey (or sufficient pieces for 4 people)	8 slices cooked turkey (or sufficient pieces for 4 people)
1 medium onion	1 medium onion
1oz butter	25g butter
½-¾oz flour	15-20g flour
¾ pint turkey stock	425ml turkey stock
2 teaspoons tomato purée	2 teaspoons tomato purée
½ teaspoon mixed herbs	½ teaspoon mixed herbs
salt	salt
pepper	pepper
1 tablespoon sherry or brandy	1 tablespoon sherry or brandy
4 tablespoons chestnut purée	4 tablespoons chestnut purée
a few chopped cooked chestnuts (if available)	a few chopped cooked chestnuts (if available)

Serves four
Preparation time: 25 minutes
Cooking time: 10 minutes
Oven: 350°F, 180°C, Gas Mark 4

Chop the onion and fry in the melted butter gently until just beginning to turn brown. Add the flour, mix well and cook for a minute, remove from the heat and slowly blend in the stock and tomato purée, until quite smooth. Return to the heat and bring to the boil, stirring continuously. Simmer for about 5 minutes and then add the herbs, seasoning and sherry or brandy. Blend in the chestnut purée, reheat and stir well, add pieces of whole chestnut. Place the turkey in an ovenproof shallow dish and pour the sauce over. Heat through for about 10 minutes in an oven at 350°F (180°C, Gas Mark 4).

Above left: Grilled Chicken with Sour Cream Sauce
Above right: Sussex Chicken Joints
Below centre: Leftover Turkey in Chestnut Sauce

Cold Dishes

ROAST CHICKEN IN ASPIC

Imperial	Metric
3lb chicken	1.5kg chicken
1½-2oz butter	40-50g butter
sprig of rosemary	sprig of rosemary
salt	salt
pepper	pepper
2 pkts aspic savoury jelly powder	2 pkts aspic savoury jelly powder
Garnish	**Garnish**
Watercress	Watercress

Serves six
Preparation time: 30 minutes
Cooking time: 1 hour 20 minutes
Oven: 375°F, 190°C, Gas Mark 5

Rub the chicken well with butter and put a good knob of butter inside the bird with the rosemary and salt and pepper. Place the chicken in a roasting tin and cook in the oven, 375°F (190°C, Gas Mark 5) for 1¼ hours. To make sure that your chicken is browned to perfection and keeps a good shape for carving, start cooking with the bird lying on its back. After the first basting, i.e. after about 20 minutes cooking time, turn the bird on to its side. When well coloured, turn it on to the other side, baste again and continue cooking, breast side uppermost. Empty the contents of the two pkts of aspic jelly into a bowl and enough hot, not boiling, water to make up to 1 pint. Cool. When the chicken is quite cold, carve and arrange the sliced breast and joints on a serving dish. Baste with the very cold, but still liquid, aspic jelly and leave to set. Garnish with bouquets of watercress and serve with rice and a green salad.

GEFLUGELSALAT

Imperial	Metric
3lb chicken, roasted	1.5kg chicken, roasted
1 onion, finely grated	1 onion, finely grated
juice of 1 lemon	juice of 1 lemon
salt	salt
4 canned pineapple rings, drained and coarsely chopped	4 canned pineapple rings, drained and coarsely chopped
1oz toasted almonds, chopped	25g toasted almonds, chopped
6oz mushrooms, sliced	150g mushrooms, sliced
1oz butter	25g butter
10 tablespoons mayonnaise	10 tablespoons mayonnaise
1 teaspoon paprika	1 teaspoon paprika
1 pinch powdered ginger	1 pinch powdered ginger
Garnish	**Garnish**
extra toasted almonds and parsley sprigs	extra toasted almonds and parsley sprigs

Serves four
Preparation time: 45 minutes
Chill time: 1 hour

Skin and debone chicken and cut into bite-size pieces and put into a bowl with the onion, lemon juice and salt to taste. Add pineapple and almonds. Fry mushrooms in butter and leave to cool. Mix mayonnaise with paprika and ginger. Add to chicken and toss thoroughly to mix. Add cooled mushrooms. Pile in serving bowl and garnish with almonds. Cool and chill for at least one hour. Decorate with parsley around the edge of the dish. Serve with freshly made toast.

DEVILLED CHICKEN DRUMSTICKS

Imperial	Metric
8 chicken drumsticks	8 chicken drumsticks
¼ pint salad oil	150ml salad oil
2 tablespoons Worcester sauce	2 tablespoons Worcester sauce
2 rounded tablespoons tomato ketchup	2 rounded tablespoons tomato ketchup
1 level tablespoon made-up mustard	1 level tablespoon made-up mustard
1 level tablespoon French mustard	1 level tablespoon French mustard
1 level teaspoon caster sugar	1 level teaspoon caster sugar
1 level tablespoon curry powder	1 level tablespoon curry powder
salt	salt
pepper	pepper
pinch of paprika	pinch of paprika

Serves four
Preparation time: 20 minutes
            (marinating time 5 to 6 hours)
Cooking time: 30 minutes
Oven: 375°F, 190°C, Gas Mark 5

Trim the drumsticks and score each with a sharp pointed knife, cutting down to the bone in several places. Mix all the remaining ingredients together to form a marinade, whisk thoroughly, then pour over the chicken pieces, making sure that the marinade penetrates the cuts. Leave for several hours or overnight if possible. Turn and baste occasionally. Drain the chicken, place the drumsticks in a baking tin. Brush with a little of the marinade and roast in the centre of a moderately hot oven 375°F (190°C, Gas Mark 5) for about 30 minutes. Turn and brush liberally with the marinade from time to time. When the chicken is golden brown, take from the pan and leave until cold. These devilled drumsticks can be served with a cocktail dip or with a salad. Wrap a small piece of foil round each drumstick tip for decoration.

Above left: Geflugelsalat
Above right: Devilled Chicken Drumsticks
Below centre: Chicken in Aspic

CHINESE CHICKEN SALAD

Imperial	Metric
2 teaspoons oil	2 teaspoons oil
1 teaspoon sesame seeds	1 teaspoon sesame seeds
1 teaspoon finely chopped fresh root ginger	1 teaspoon finely chopped fresh root ginger
2 tablespoons soy sauce	2 tablespoons soy sauce
1 clove garlic	1 clove garlic
3 tablespoons sugar	3 tablespoons sugar
½ teaspoon mixed spices powder	½ teaspoon mixed spices powder
3lb chicken, jointed	1.5kg chicken, jointed
oil for frying	oil for frying
4 spring onions, sliced	4 spring onions, sliced
2 celery stalks, sliced	2 celery stalks, sliced
6 water chestnuts, sliced	6 water chestnuts, sliced
1 small can bamboo shoots, cut into strips	1 small can bamboo shoots, cut into strips
salt	salt
pepper	pepper
6-8 lettuce leaves	6-8 lettuce leaves

Serves four
Preparation and cooking time: 1 hour 30 minutes

Heat 2 teaspoons oil, add sesame seeds and fry until golden brown. Drain on kitchen paper. Mix ginger, soy sauce, garlic, sugar and half the mixed spices powder together. Pour over the chicken joints and set aside for 20 minutes. Drain the chicken joints, then deep fry for 5-8 minutes or until they are cooked through and tender. Drain on kitchen paper and leave until cool enough to handle. Remove meat from bones and cut into strips. Chill for 15 minutes. Add the onions, celery, water chestnuts and bamboo shoots to the chicken strips. Season with remaining mixed spices powder and salt and pepper to taste. Line a bowl with lettuce leaves and spoon the chicken mixture into the centre. Sprinkle over a little oil and the sesame seeds.

DANISH STYLE CHICKEN SALAD

Imperial	Metric
12-16oz cooked chicken	350-450g cooked chicken
4 hardboiled eggs	4 hardboiled eggs
1½ tablespoons freshly grated horseradish OR 2 tablespoons horseradish and cream sauce	1½ tablespoons freshly grated horseradish OR 2 tablespoons horseradish and cream sauce
½ tablespoon vinegar or lemon juice	½ tablespoon vinegar or lemon juice
6 tablespoons whipped cream	6 tablespoons whipped cream
salt	salt
pepper	pepper
1 bunch watercress or parsley sprigs	1 bunch watercress or parsley sprigs

Serves four
Preparation time: 25 to 30 minutes

Cut the chicken into cubes. Shell the eggs, chop finely or mash with a fork. To the chopped or mashed eggs add horseradish, vinegar or lemon juice and mix. Blend in the cream. Add chicken and seasoning to taste and stir well. Pile onto a dish and surround with watercress or parsley sprigs.

Left: Chinese Chicken Salad
Centre: Danish Style Chicken Salad
Right: Chicken Quiche

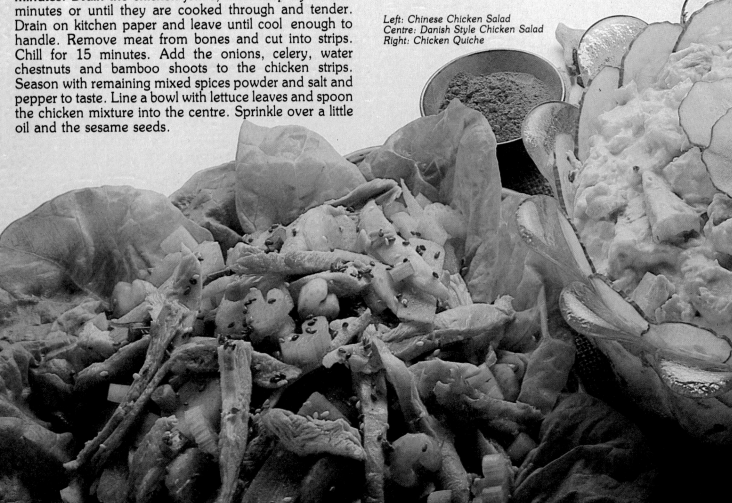

CHICKEN QUICHE

Imperial	Metric
2oz rice	50g rice
2oz cooked peas	50g cooked peas
2oz cooked, diced carrots	50g cooked, diced carrots
oil and vinegar dressing	oil and vinegar dressing
1 shortcrust pastry flan case, baked blind	1 shortcrust pastry flan case, baked blind
2oz cooked chicken, minced or diced	50g cooked chicken, minced or diced
mayonnaise	mayonnaise
2 tomatoes, sliced	2 tomatoes, sliced
1 hardboiled egg, sliced	1 hardboiled egg, sliced

Garnish

stuffed olives
radishes
watercress

Serves four to six
Preparation time: 45 minutes

Boil the rice in salted water until tender. Rinse under cold tap, drain and dry it. Mix with the cooked peas and carrots. Make some dressing by mixing 2 teaspoons of olive oil with 1 teaspoon of vinegar, season and mix well. Toss the rice and vegetables in the dressing and spread across the bottom of the flan. Next, spread the minced or diced chicken over the rice mixture, and coat very sparingly with mayonnaise. Top with sliced tomatoes and hardboiled egg, also sliced. Garnish with halved stuffed olives or halved radishes and sprigs of watercress. Serve with lettuce and cucumber.

PEACHY CHICKEN SALAD

Imperial	Metric
8oz chicken, cooked	225g chicken, cooked
8oz celery, diced	225g celery, diced
8oz peaches, sliced	225g peaches, sliced
1 tablespoon onion, chopped	1 tablespoon onion, chopped
salt	salt
pepper	pepper
juice of ½ lemon	juice of ½ lemon
lettuce leaves	lettuce leaves
4oz cooked rice	100g cooked rice
a few slivered almonds	a few slivered almonds

Sour Cream Dressing	**Sour Cream Dressing**
¼ pint sour cream	150ml sour cream
3 tablespoons lemon juice	3 tablespoons lemon juice
pinch of salt	pinch of salt
pinch of paprika	pinch of paprika
¼ teaspoon dry mustard	¼ teaspoon dry mustard
1 tablespoon onion, finely chopped	1 tablespoon onion, finely chopped

Serves four
Preparation time: 30 minutes

Cut the chicken into cubes and mix with the diced celery and sliced peaches. Stir in the chopped onion, season with salt and pepper and sprinkle with lemon juice. Arrange well-washed and dried lettuce leaves on a flat serving dish. Mix the cold rice with some of the sour cream dressing, and place a little on each leaf. Toss the chicken mixture in the rest of the sour cream dressing and arrange the mixture on top of the lettuce salad. Sprinkle with slivered almonds. *To make sour cream dressing:* Whip the cream, add all the other ingredients and mix thoroughly.

CHICKEN MAYONNAISE

Imperial	Metric
3lb chicken	1.5kg chicken
butter	butter
¼ pint mayonnaise	150ml mayonnaise
1 onion, finely chopped	1 onion, finely chopped
2oz gherkins, finely chopped	50g gherkins, finely chopped
2oz capers, finely chopped	50g capers, finely chopped
½oz parsley, chopped	15g parsley, chopped
½oz gelatine	15g gelatine

Garnish	**Garnish**
potato crisps	potato crisps
sliced cucumber	sliced cucumber
sliced pimento	sliced pimento

Serves six
Preparation time: 45 minutes
Cooking time: 1 hour 20 minutes
Oven: 375°F, 190°C, Gas Mark 5

Left: Chicken Mayonnaise
Centre: Peachy Chicken Salad
Right: Picnic Pie

Rub the chicken well with butter and wrap in aluminium foil. Cook in the oven 375°F (190°C, Gas Mark 5) for 1 hour and 20 minutes. Allow to cool. When the chicken is quite cold, remove the skin, carve and arrange the portions on a serving dish. Blend the mayonnaise with the onion, gherkins, capers and parsley. Make up the gelatine according to packet instructions and stir in the mayonnaise. When on the point of setting, spoon the mayonnaise over the chicken portions. Decorate with potato crisps, sliced cucumber and pimento.

PICNIC PIE

Imperial	Metric
Pastry	**Pastry**
12oz flour	350g flour
3oz lard or vegetable fat	75g lard or vegetable fat
3oz margarine	75g margarine
pinch of salt	pinch of salt
about 3 tablespoons cold water	about 3 tablespoons cold water
Filling	**Filling**
8oz chicken, cooked and diced	225g chicken, cooked and diced
2oz ham, cooked and diced	50g ham, cooked and diced
8oz cooked peas and carrots or any suitable cooked vegetables	225g cooked peas and carrots or any suitable cooked vegetables
1 onion, finely chopped or grated	1 onion, finely chopped or grated
2-3 tablespoons mayonnaise	2-3 tablespoons mayonnaise
salt	salt
pepper	pepper
Glaze	**Glaze**
milk or beaten egg	milk or beaten egg

Serves five to six
Preparation time: 30 minutes
Cooking time: 30 minutes
Oven: 400°F, 200°C, Gas Mark 6

Make shortcrust pastry, knead well and divide into two-thirds and one-third. Roll out the larger piece and line an 8-9 inch (20-22.5cm) ovenproof flan ring. Prick base with a fork. Mix the filling ingredients together and place in pastry case. Dampen the edges of the pastry. Roll out remaining pastry and place over filling, pressing the edges of pastry together well. Trim off any excess and flute the edges. Use trimmings to make leaves for top. Brush over top with milk or beaten egg and make a hole with a skewer in centre of pie to let steam escape. Bake at 400°F (200°C, Gas Mark 6) for about 30 minutes until golden brown. Cool on wire rack, then chill in refrigerator. Serve either with a mixed salad or with whole tomatoes and cos lettuce leaves.

JELLIED CHICKEN RING

Imperial	Metric
1oz gelatine	25g gelatine
¾ pint chicken stock	425ml chicken stock
1 tablespoon lemon juice	1 tablespoon lemon juice
7 tablespoons vinegar	7 tablespoons vinegar
2 tablespoons tomato juice	2 tablespoons tomato juice
1 teaspoon sugar	1 teaspoon sugar
salt	salt
pepper	pepper
¾lb cooked and diced chicken	350g cooked and diced chicken
small pkt frozen peas, cooked	small pkt frozen peas, cooked
½lb diced cooked carrots	225g diced cooked carrots

Serves four
Preparation time: 30 minutes

Dissolve gelatine in a little boiling water, add stock then lemon juice, vinegar, tomato juice, sugar and seasoning. Cool, put a thin layer in a jelly ring, allow to set. Mix together ½lb (225g) of the diced chicken with the vegetables. Fold into the rest of the jelly when it begins to thicken. Put into the ring and set. Turn out and fill the centre with the rest of the chicken. Garnish with lettuce, tomatoes and watercress.

CURRIED CHICKEN SALAD WITH SAFFRON RICE

Imperial	Metric
1oz butter or margarine	25g butter or margarine
1oz plain flour	25g plain flour
½ pint milk	300ml milk
¼ pint chicken stock — cubes can be used	150ml chicken stock — cubes can be used
1 teaspoon curry powder	1 teaspoon curry powder
salt	salt
½ teaspoon paprika	½ teaspoon paprika
grated rind of 1 lemon	grated rind of 1 lemon
¼ pint single cream	150ml single cream
2oz raisins	50g raisins
8oz cooked, diced chicken	225g cooked, diced chicken
Saffron Rice	**Saffron Rice**
8oz long grain rice	225g long grain rice
1 teaspoon saffron	1 teaspoon saffron
salt	salt
chopped parsley to garnish	chopped parsley to garnish

Serves eight
Preparation and cooking time: 25 minutes

Melt fat, stir in flour and cook for 1-2 minutes. Gradually blend in milk and chicken stock and heat, stirring continuously until boiling and thickened. Simmer for further 1-2 minutes, add curry powder, salt to taste, paprika and lemon rind. Allow to cool a little, then beat in

the cream until smooth. Add the raisins, then the diced chicken and combine well. Cook the rice with the saffron in plenty of boiling salted water until tender, 12-15 minutes. Drain and rinse well in cold water. When well drained, pile around the edge of the serving dish and heap the chicken mixture in the centre. Garnish with chopped parsley.

or skewers. Put the chicken in a large saucepan and pour in enough water to cover. Add the vinegar and sugar and bring to the boil. Cover and simmer for about 1½ hours or until chicken is tender. Cool the chicken in the liquid, then carve with the stuffing and serve cold with a tossed green salad and a potato mayonnaise salad.

HINDLE WAKES

Imperial	Metric
4lb chicken	1.75kg chicken
4fl oz vinegar	125ml vinegar
1 tablespoon sugar	1 tablespoon sugar
Stuffing	**Stuffing**
8oz prunes, soaked, stoned and chopped	225g prunes, soaked, stoned and chopped
2oz shredded suet	50g shredded suet
2oz fresh breadcrumbs	50g fresh breadcrumbs
1 teaspoon grated lemon rind	1 teaspoon grated lemon rind
2 teaspoons chopped parsley	2 teaspoons chopped parsley
salt	salt
pepper	pepper

Serves four to five
Preparation time: 15 minutes
Cooking time: 1 hour 30 minutes

Mix the stuffing ingredients together and fill the cavity of the chicken with the mixture. Secure the cavity with string

Left: Jellied Chicken Ring
Centre: Curried Chicken Salad with Saffron Rice
Right: Hindle Wakes

TURKEY AND YOGHURT SALAD

Imperial	Metric
12oz turkey, cooked	350g turkey, cooked
½ cucumber, sliced	½ cucumber, sliced
Dressing	**Dressing**
¼ pint yoghurt	125ml yoghurt
1 tablespoon chives, chopped	1 tablespoon chives, chopped
¼ teaspoon dry mustard	¼ teaspoon dry mustard
¼ teaspoon garlic salt	¼ teaspoon garlic salt
1 teaspoon vinegar or lemon juice	1 teaspoon vinegar or lemon juice
salt	salt
pepper	pepper

Serves four
Preparation time: 20 minutes

Cut the turkey and cucumber into small strips and mix together in a bowl. Prepare the dressing by mixing all the ingredients together. Add to the turkey and cucumber. Toss lightly. Serve on lettuce leaves, and garnish with sliced tomatoes.

EASTERN TURKEY SALAD

Imperial	Metric
4oz green grapes	100g green grapes
8oz turkey, cooked and diced	225g turkey, cooked and diced
4oz rice, boiled	100g rice, boiled
1 stick celery, diced	1 stick celery, diced
2oz sauteed fresh mushrooms	50g sauteed fresh mushrooms
8 black olives, stoned and chopped	8 black olives, stoned and chopped
4 tablespoons oil	4 tablespoons oil
2 tablespoons vinegar	2 tablespoons vinegar
2 teaspoons onion juice	2 teaspoons onion juice
¼ teaspoon rosemary	¼ teaspoon rosemary
¼ teaspoon pepper	¼ teaspoon pepper
1 teaspoon salt	1 teaspoon salt

Serves four
Preparation time: 30 minutes

Remove the pips from the grapes. Mix together the diced turkey, rice, diced celery, mushrooms, olives and grapes. Thoroughly shake together the oil, vinegar, onion juice, rosemary, pepper and salt and pour over the turkey mixture. Serve very cold on a bed of shredded lettuce.

TURKEY AND CELERY SALAD

Imperial	Metric
3lb turkey, cooked and the meat cut into small pieces	1.5kg turkey, cooked and the meat cut into small pieces
1 stick celery, finely chopped	1 stick celery, finely chopped
2oz smoked ham chopped, for garnish	50g smoked ham chopped, for garnish
Dressing	**Dressing**
4 tablespoons salad oil, preferably olive oil	4 tablespoons salad oil, preferably olive oil
2 tablespoons white wine vinegar	2 tablespoon white wine vinegar
salt	salt
pepper	pepper
pinch of mustard	pinch of mustard
½ teaspoon sugar	½ teaspoon sugar
2 teaspoons chives, chopped	2 teaspoons chives, chopped

Serves four
Preparation time: 1 hour 10 minutes

Put turkey and celery into a bowl, cover and chill for one hour. Make dressing: put oil, vinegar and seasonings in a screw top jar and shake vigorously. Pour over turkey and celery, add chopped chives and mix well so as to coat the pieces with the dressing. Transfer the salad to a bowl or dish and garnish with the chopped ham.

Above centre: Eastern Turkey Salad
Below left: Turkey and Yoghurt Salad
Below right: Turkey and Celery Salad

Index

Acknowledgments

The Publishers would like to thank
the following for their kindness in
providing materials and equipment
used in the photography of this
book:
Richard Dare, D.H. Evans
Department Store, John Lewis
Department Store, David Mellor
and Harvey Nichols & Company
Ltd.

Designed by Wensley Bown,
Chesham
Photography by Paul Kemp.

Produced in association with the
Buxted Advisory Service and
McGougan Advertising.